WHAT ABOUT **THE RUSSIANS?**

A Christian Approach to U.S. — Soviet Conflict

Edited by Dale W. Brown

THE BRETHREN PRESS
Elgin, Illinois

© 1984 by The Brethren Press

The Brethren Press, 1451 Dundee Avenue, Elgin, IL 60120

Cover design by Kathy Kline

Photo credits: Clyde Weaver and David Morris

Edited by Leslie R. Keylock

Library of Congress Cataloging in Publication Data

What about the Russians?

Bibliography: p. 156
1. United States—Foreign relations—Soviet Union—Addresses, essays, lectures. 2. Soviet Union—Foreign relations—United States—Addresses, essays, lectures. 3. Christianity and international affairs—Addresses, essays, lectures. I. Brown, Dale W., 1926-
E183.8.S65W46 1984   327.73047   84-6169
ISBN 0-87178-751-2

CONTENTS

INTRODUCTION

Russians often boast that there are more teachers of English in the Soviet Union than students of the Russian language in the United States. This fact suggests that they are more interested in us than we are in them.

Whatever the truth of this claim, it is disturbing how little the peoples of the two "superpowers" know about each other. Our strong feelings about Russia, good and bad, have too often emerged from superficial and prejudicial information, lacking basic study and application of the golden rule. In his excellent contribution to this anthology, lay Orthodox theologian Anthony Ugolnik warns that the American church is held hostage by its ignorance of its Russian counterpart.

How much do we know about life in the massive land area that stretches seven thousand miles from the borders of Poland to the shores of the Pacific? How well do we understand the nearly three hundred million people who make up the Union of Soviet Socialist Republics, a federation of sixteen diverse republics. It is important to recognize that the Russians constitute about fifty percent of the total population. For the sake of simplicity, our authors follow popular usage in employing "Russian" as a generic term, one that encompasses a great plurality of ethnic, religious, and linguistic groups. Few Americans realize that there are more Muslims in the Soviet Union than in Egypt, which is from eighty-six to ninety percent Muslim. Asiatic Russia includes a fascinating mixture of Buddhist, Hindu, tribal, and racial enclaves.

This common lack of basic knowledge and understanding is all the more startling in light of the fact that for the rest of the century world peace and human survival will depend to a considerable extent on the ability of the Soviet Union and the United States to deal with the growing sense of conflict. The aggressive nature of the rivalry means that the eruption of violence any place in the world makes possible a dangerous confrontation between the superpowers.

The rhetoric of our political climate reflects a pervasive fear of the Russians. Conversations with Soviet citizens reveal their great fear of outsiders, including China, Western Europe, and America.

On both sides of the "Iron Curtain" the fears of the other side seem to border on paranoia. Some of the fears are justified, but others are not. There are increasing numbers sharing a worldwide fear, the fear that our fears of one another are pushing us toward the precipice of mutual suicide. In his farewell address to the American people President Eisenhower spoke eloquently against such pervasive fear:

> Down the long lane of history yet to be written, America knows that this world of ours, ever growing smaller, must avoid becoming a community of dreadful fear and hate, and be, instead, a proud confederation of mutual trust and respect.

It is hoped that this book will contribute to new beginnings in understanding the peoples of the Soviet Union. Whether the reader agrees with all of the authors or not, it is anticipated that the essays will contribute to honest dialogue both within and between our countries. As Christians we pray that the book will foster the kind of mutual trust Eisenhower saw as "a continuing imperative." The more we listened to the news as we gathered material from those who knew the American-Soviet conflict intimately, the more relevant this book has seemed to be.

A basic issue emerged early in the project. Would our writers be sufficiently critical of Soviet policies? Some contributors maintained that harsh attacks would accomplish little apart from bolstering our already inflated sense of self-righteousness. In fact, they might jeopardize chances of changes for the better. Others argued, however, that a Christian approach must be boldly prophetic in speaking the truth to powers and principalities. True peace can only come through a realistic assessment of other nations. In spite of these differences, however, the authors represent broadly what may be called a moderate position. Such a stance can neither be described as a polemical tirade against everything Russian or a naïve whitewash of Soviet policies.

Some of the writers and many of our readers will judge parts of this anthology as too "hawkish." Others will say much of the content is "dovish." It is too much to expect that the authors will completely agree with one another or speak with equal relevance to the basic questions.

In spite of the limitations, though, an anthology does have certain advantages. One can profit from selected essays without the necessity of reading what comes before. Differing opinions might contribute to confusion more than to understanding. On the other hand different accents might help compose a symphony of deeper understanding. Many of our Russian friends will not agree with all the impressions and interpretations.

As we have thought about the book, we have wondered what might be said in a book from Russia entitled *What About The Americans?* If such a book is written, it could certainly contain some views offensive to our ears.

The anthology is unapologetically Christian. This does not mean the authors lack adequate credentials to write about American-Soviet relationships. Most brought to their writing a rich background of direct contacts with the Soviet people. Several are highly qualified Kremlinologists. But the book is different than most in its effort to examine the conflict from a Christian perspective. Most of the writers speak out of biblical and theological imperatives that shape their responses. It is hoped, however, that in speaking clearly to a Christian audience, the book will also speak to the consciences of all who are struggling with one of the most crucial issues of our day. The questions posed in the chapter titles are those a great majority of Americans are asking.

Credit for the idea of the book belongs to Clyde Weaver, marketing director of The Brethren Press. His interest was engendered through his participation in the Moscow International Book Fairs of 1981 and 1983 and his many conversations with the Soviet people. Robert C. Johansen of the Institute for World Order gave invaluable counsel as to format and potential writers. Through the many contacts I made during the preparation of this anthology, I have become aware anew of the number and quality of people who are deeply concerned about this issue. It has been a source of joy and hope to come into close contact with the renewed interest in Russian studies, many plans for direct people-to-people exchanges, and widespread motivation to participate in whatever ways possible in the Pauline wish to "break down the dividing walls of hostility" between our two peoples.

Dale W. Brown
Bethany Theological Seminary

Part I

WHO ARE THE RUSSIANS?

It was in Russia that I experienced the kind of genuine and warm hospitality reminiscent of my Midwest boyhood. It was in greeting Orthodox priests that I really practiced what had been a part of my sectarian heritage, namely, the biblical admonition to greet one another with the holy kiss. The only place in the world where I was treated as royalty occurred in the citadel of the proletariat. At the same time I had the uncomfortable feeling that if I lived there my radical peace church position might get me in difficulty. Though I am not mystically inclined, the choral music of Orthodoxy transported me to seventh heaven. And the gentle homilies of the clergy were so much like the admonitions of John's Gospel to love one another I heard from the benches of our little church. It was in the Soviet Union that I was forced to deal with the materialism of my culture, as well as theirs. Overall, I experienced the riddle, the mystery, the paradox that is Russia. It is this enigma and lack of understanding that Rolf Theen highlights in the first essay.

The contacts and conversations that shaped this anthology opened a floodgate to these many memories of my own visit. Though hosted by the Russian Orthodox Church, our Brethren delegation was free to plan a variety of experiences. I remember the large portion of a day we spent at the University of Moscow, a high-rise with over 35,000 students. As congenial professors shared about their life in academia, I was struck by the similarities with the ethos of scientism, materialism, and service of national needs that permeate our own institutions. I thought of Jacques Ellul, who judges America and the Soviet Union to be the two most alike nations in the world. Both exemplify his analysis of technique, the conjoining of huge state bureaucracies, corporate management of technology, and militarism.

However, it is Professor Theen's concern to document the differences as well as the similarities. He calls peacemakers to be realistic about Soviet ideology and practice. As a political scientist he focuses more on the background of the present political milieu than on the culture, everyday life, and aspirations of the people. Other writers will balance his focus in their portrayals of the people. Nevertheless, Theen supports the strong consensus that emerges in the anthology, one that asserts that in spite of their differences Christians should seek reconciliation with the Soviet peoples and their government.

I remember an unforgettable experience at Zagorsk, the Vatican of Russian Orthodoxy. With its multitude of churches and onion domes, healing waters, and large trees in autumn splendor, I judged Zagorsk to be one of the most picturesque places in the world. We stood for hours in worship, were privileged to meet the patriarch, visited the rector of the theological seminary, and were inspired by the spontaneous worship of thousands of pilgrims who had made their way to celebrate St. Sergius's day. After the great day I was favored with a small room in the the monastery. I crawled into bed. Quickly my consciousness of the holy place combined with the ethereal music, flickering candle, and illuminated icon to pull me out of bed to kneel in prayer.

I sensed with Paul Vallière the great reservoir of spirituality that survives alongside official atheistic ideology. At Zagorsk I realized, as I had in viewing the architectural and art treasures in the Kremlin, that the Orthodox Church provides one of the main links with the past. The second chapter is helpful in dealing with the conflict between the Russian tradition of spirituality and Marxist ideology. Whenever Soviet society is perceived to be in a state of bad health, one of the ways to protest is to identify with the best from the past. As a result of standing for hours in crowded churches, I agree with Vallière's conclusion: "Whenever and wherever the day of reform dawns in the Soviet system, religion will be a part of it. . . . "

What Vallière writes about as an empathetic Protestant, Anthony Ugolnik describes from the point of view of an insider, one deeply immersed in the Orthodox tradition. Though born an American in Detroit, Professor Ugolnik visits Russia as one who knows their language and tradition. He identifies with the faith and life of believers, often without their being aware he is an American. For this reason his portraits of individual Russians are the most beautiful and revealing I have encountered. We are fortunate to have his contribution and are indebted to him and the editors of Sojourners for permission to use his revision of an article that appeared in the November 1982 issue. The remaining essays about the people are by those who have journeyed to the Soviet Union for special reasons. You will discover their deep love for the people.

1

WHAT ARE THE ROOTS
OF TODAY'S RUSSIA?

Rolf H. W. Theen

In a radio broadcast in 1939, Sir Winston Churchill described Russia as "a riddle, wrapped in a mystery, inside an enigma." There is little question that today, some forty-five years later, this intriguing bit of prose remains for most Americans an apt description of a country they have great difficulty understanding.

The general public in the United States has been unable to comprehend the "uncertain colossus",[1] that has fundamentally altered America's sense of national priorities and probably permanently deflected the course of American history from its trajectory of development at the end of World War II. The same must be said, by and large, of its political leadership. F. D. Roosevelt, earnestly but naïvely believed in the possibility of great power cooperation after the war and, in particular, in continued United States – Soviet collaboration. From then on to the belligerent rhetoric and assertive political stance of the Reagan administration, American political leaders have tended to perceive the Soviet Union as either (1) a responsible member of the international community, (2) a country that can and should be engaged through trade, cultural exchange, and negotiations of various sorts, or (3) a more or less demoniac force that must be resisted and contained at all costs. Occasionally they have even contrived to do all three at the same time.

The public image of Russia has fluctuated widely and rapidly in the United States – more so than in any other Western country. With few exceptions, the American news media tend to ignore the Soviet Union. Measured by its intrinsic importance, coverage of the history, culture, and peoples of the largest country on earth certainly has been, and continues to be, woefully inadequate. As a result, our image of Russia tends to be a collage of crisis situations. Then coverage of the Soviet Union in the news media suddenly expands in mushroom-like fashion but is not always at its best in terms of quality.

Given the frequency and the enormous parameters of the unexpected swings in the public image of the Soviet Union in the United States, as well as the inherent contradictions in this image at any given time, it is no wonder that Americans are confused about Russia.

Things are not much more encouraging when one turns to an examination of American scholarly literature on Russia and the Soviet Union. American specialists on the Soviet Union and its historic predecessor frequently exhibit similar fluctuations and wide disagreements in their writings. This fact is exemplified currently in the work of Princeton's George F. Kennan, former United States ambassador to the Soviet Union, and Harvard's Richard Pipes, presently a member of the United States National Security Council.[2]

In 1958, Daniel Bell wrote his famous essay, "Ten Theories in Search of Reality." It was an attempt to come to grips with the plethora of different approaches to the study of Russia and the Soviet Union then identifiable in the work of specialists.[3]

During the past thirty-five years, a great deal of new blood has been added to the ranks of scholars specializing in Soviet studies. Were Daniel Bell to write a similar essay today, he would have to add many more approaches to his list of "theories."

The point is that no consensus has emerged in American scholarly literature on Russia and the Soviet Union. As a matter of fact, one can detect the same pattern of differing perspectives and extreme swings even within the work of some individuals. G. F. Kennan, who in 1947 stated an eloquent argument for the containment of the Soviet Union,[4] has of late made an equally eloquent case against any American policy toward the Soviet Union based primarily on military strength, including continued reliance on nuclear deterrence. The evolution of Kennan's thinking on American — Soviet relations, it goes without saying, is the result of many factors. They include his own changing perception of American policy and the realities of power politics in the nuclear age. But presumably his changed viewpoint also reflects a different perspective on the Soviet Union, a perspective that emphasizes the change of the Soviet system since the days of Stalin. His current prescriptions certainly would be difficult to reconcile with his analysis of the Soviet system laid out in the "X" article of 1947, which gives a very negative evaluation of that system.

A large part of the problem involved in trying to understand Russia and the Soviet Union, it goes without saying, has to do with the intrinsic difficulty of the subject matter. More than a century ago, the Russian poet F. I. Tiutchev wrote:

> One cannot understand Russia with the mind alone,
> She cannot be measured with an ordinary yardstick:
> She is unique and stands alone —
> One can only believe in Russia.[5]

Tiutchev notwithstanding, there is a great deal about Russia and its modern variant, the Soviet Union, that can be learned and understood. On the other hand, the poet is undoubtedly right in suggesting that the sum total of our knowledge does not add up to a complete understanding of Russia. She cannot be fathomed with ordinary measures.

Like the United States, historic Russia may be regarded as a cultural outpost of Europe. The historical evolution of these two offshoots of European civilization, however, turned out to be very different. By the end of the eighteenth century America had come to represent a new extreme of liberty. At the same time Russia had generated a new extreme of despotism. Both of these extremes challenged the ancien régime of Europe and ultimately contributed to its downfall.

The story of the subsequent confrontation of America and Russia is familiar. After World War I it manifested itself on the ideological plane — an encounter personified, as George F. Kennan has suggested, in the figures of Wilson and Lenin.[6] The Second World War resulted in the unexpected spectacle of the United States and the Soviet Union facing each other across a devastated, demoralized, and disintegrated Europe. As is well known, in its subsequent development the confrontation between the United States and the Soviet Union transcended the bounds of an ideological encounter and assumed the dimensions of a political, economic, and military struggle between East and West.

Like the United States, Russia is a country in whose history the presence of the frontier played an important role. Following its own version of "manifest destiny," as it were, Russia expanded eastward to the Pacific and southward into Central Asia and the Middle East. In the process it created the largest country on earth with contiguous territory. However, while America's territorial expansion came to an end at the shores of the Pacific, the expansion of Russia and its successor, the Soviet Union, has continued to our day. In the course of World War II, for example, the Soviet Union added some 265,000 square miles to its territory — an area large enough to accommodate all of Norway, Poland, and Costa Rica, or almost all of Texas. As a result, the Soviet Union today is considerably larger than its predecessor, the Russian Empire, was at its zenith in 1904.

Moreover, although in the course of their historical evolution and territorial expansion both America and Russia produced societies with populations characterized by a high degree of ethnic heterogeneity and cultural diversity, America gave rise to a more unified civilization than did Russia. While sizable concentrations of ethnic groups and significant cultural differences continue to exist in segments of the American population, they are not nearly so pronounced as those one encounters in the Soviet Union today. Both the United States and the Soviet Union are blessed with rich natural and human resources — resources that are certainly enormous by the standards of the European and most other countries. Both societies have a deep interest in education and a strong commitment to the development of science and technology, as well as social progress — at least at the ideological level.

In both the Soviet Union and the United States one can find the same (or a similar) curious mixture of materialism and idealism, as well as a profound skepticism toward the ways of the Old World. In the twentieth century both countries emerged as champions of national self-determination and advocates of a new international order. . . .

The list of similarities between America and Russia could, no doubt, be extended considerably. Upon closer examination, however, many of these similarities turn out to be more apparent than real. The fact is that, in spite of a good many profound and superficial similarities, the United States and Russia in many respects represent societies whose cultural values and heritage, economic system, and political institutions are fundamentally different and even diametrically opposed. Nothing is to be gained by ignoring or overlooking these differences. As a matter of fact, it seems to me, any meaningful and ultimately successful attempt to define possible areas of agreement and common ground between the two societies must proceed from a full appreciation of the enormous differences between them.

Through the adoption of the Greek Orthodox faith from Constantinople in the tenth century, Russia effectively cut itself off from the rest of Europe, as Peter Chaadayev pointed out in his *Philosophical Letters* (1823-31).[7] The main contacts with the outside world the emerging Russia developed were not with Western

Europe but with the Byzantine Empire, located in the area now occupied by Turkey. The "Byzantine connection" in Russian history, inter alia, resulted in the growing isolation of Russia from the mainstream of European history for a number of centuries. This isolation was reinforced by the Mongol conquest and domination of most of Russia for some two hundred years, beginning in the thirteenth century.[8]

As a result, such important movements in history as the Renaissance and the Reformation were to have no impact on Russia. Eventually, Russia's Byzantine heritage would include Orthodox Christianity instead of Roman Catholicism, the Cyrillic instead of the Latin alphabet, and the institution and concept of the "tsar" — a kind of God-Emperor who in his person combined both supreme spiritual authority and supreme secular power — instead of a limited or constitutional monarchy.

From Byzantium, furthermore, Russia inherited a "singularly conservative, anti-intellectual, and xenophobic ethos."[9] Russia, as a matter of fact, laid explicit claim to the religious and political heritage of Byzantium. After the Turks conquered Constantinople, the capital of the Byzantine Empire, in 1453, the Grand Dukes of Moscow adopted the Byzantine double-headed eagle as their insignia and assumed the title of "tsar." Moscow was officially proclaimed the "Third Rome." The idea was that, as a result of the fall of Constantinople, the "Second Rome," the center of Christianity had once again shifted to the East, and Moscow had now become the sole repository of the true Christian faith, and it would henceforth remain the center of Orthodoxy.

The idea that Moscow was the new and permanent center of Christianity, the final home of Orthodoxy, played an important role in the formation of the Muscovite state. It imbued it with a strong and growing sense of messianism and reinforced its isolation from Europe.[10] The profession of *pravoslavie*, i.e., the true, Orthodox faith, became the decisive test of belonging to the Russian kingdom. There are some striking and instructive parallels for us to ponder in the proclamation and enforcement, some centuries later, of a modern type of "Orthodoxy," viz., Moscow's version of Communism. In Stalin's Russia, too, it was the profession of the only true faith, i.e., Communism as interpreted ultimately by Stalin himself, that determined membership in the Soviet orbit and the world of "proletarian revolutionary internationalism." In the show trials of the 1930s Stalin's political opponents were tried for various forms of "heresy." To this day "revisionism" of any sort remains one of the cardinal sins in the Communist world.

In any event, as the result of its isolation from the West, Russia remained largely unaffected by the intellectual and spiritual movements that provided the basis of the modernization and secularization of Europe. When the West came to Russia in the fifteenth century, it encountered a civilization ill-prepared to cope with the vastly more advanced world of Europe. The result was a deep crisis of identity, akin to the trauma of adolescence. Like the underdeveloped countries in our time, the emerging Russia was forced into a search for national identity in what was then an essentially European world. And as in the case of many underdeveloped countries today, the Russian reaction to Europe was highly ambivalent. In the words of one Western historian, "The Russian response to the inescapable challenge of Western Europe was split—almost schizophrenic—and this division has to some extent lasted down to the present."[11]

It was, however, not until the seventeenth century that a far-reaching process of selective Westernization began in Russia—a process that, as it turned out, called forth an enormously powerful reaction. The reign of Peter the Great, which was marked by an unprecedented policy of forced Westernization, now constitutes the great "divide" in Russian history. This fact is reflected in the distinction Russian historians commonly make between pre-Petrine and post-Petrine Russia.

What is more, the forced selective Westernization of Russia under Peter the Great made the question of Russia's relationship to the West into the central and most crucial issue of a national debate. That debate has gone on ever since. Perhaps future historians will look upon the Russian Revolution of 1917 as merely one chapter in this debate—and not necessarily the concluding one.

This ambivalence of their attitude toward the West, we might note, has not remained a secret to the Russians. In his novel *Smoke,* written in 1867, I. S. Turgenev, for example, tells us that whenever ten or so Russians meet together, "they immediately begin to discuss the question of the significance and the future of Russia. . . . They chew and chew on that unfortunate question like children chew on a piece of rubber: no juice, no taste. And, of course, they will take a stab at the rotten West. . . . It's a curious thing. . . . This West defeats us on every point—yet we declare that it is rotten! And if we only had genuine contempt for it. . . . However, all that is nothing but phrases and lies. We abuse and criticize it, and yet we value only its opinions."[12]

Turgenev was merely echoing ideas concerning Russia's relationship to Europe that had been an integral part of Russian thought and intellectual life for some time. In the 1830s P. Ia. Chaadayev had first raised the fateful question of the destiny of Russia, its place in world history, and its relationship to the West. He emphasized, on the one hand, Russia's backwardness and its "feeble link" to Europe, to whom it stood (and should stand) in the relationship of an apprentice. But he also predicted that Russia was destined to teach Europe "an infinity of things she could not conceive without us." Ultimately, it would be Russia's role and mission to "resolve most of the social problems, to perfect most of the ideas that have come up in the old societies, and to decide most of the weighty questions concerning the human race." This would be the "logical result of our long solitude," Chaadayev wrote, for "great things have always come from the desert."[13]

The publication of Chaadayev's *Philosophical Letters* in 1836 called forth the "great debate" between the so-called *zapadniki* (those Russians who identified with Europe and argued that Russia was destined to follow the example of Europe) and the Slavophiles (those Russians who rejected the West and believed in Russia's uniqueness and special destiny).

However, it should be pointed out that even the *zapadniki* or Westernizers found it difficult to accept the West as it then existed. Their thoughts and ideas were largely shaped by those Western intellectual currents that were critical of the social and political status quo in Europe. They were greatly influenced by the writings of the utopian socialists—Proudhon, St. Simon, Fourier, and Robert Owen—and oriented their thinking toward a postbourgeois or postcapitalist Europe.

In short, the sense of affinity among the *zapadniki* for the common destiny of Russia and Europe involved an identification not with the "old," existing, bourgeois Europe, but with the "new," future, socialist Europe, a Europe that had yet to be born.

The traditional ambivalence in the Russian attitude toward the West is readily observable today. As anyone who has traveled extensively in the Soviet Union can attest, Russian interest in the West (and particularly in America) is far greater than Western or American interest in Russia. But nearly seven decades after the October Revolution, Russians still look on the "old world" of Europe "with hatred, and with love"—to use the language of Alexander Blok's poem *The Scythians,* written in 1918. The ambivalence and mixed emotions noted by Turgenev and Blok today find expression in countless anecdotes circulating in the Soviet Union. They are also reflected in the questions Russians cautiously put to Westerners when they feel at ease and unobserved—questions that are most revealing in regard to what Russians know and do not know about the West, as well as in regard to what they think of us and how they perceive us.

In the presence of foreigners, Russians will often despise and condemn the West because of its materialism, its frequent indecision and vacillation, its lack of moral values and civic responsibility, its blatant socioeconomic inequality, its racism, and its militarism.

On the other hand, Western visitors to the Soviet Union frequently encounter among Russians an enormous admiration for Western science and technology, economic efficiency, and standard of living. Frequently their imagination is electrified in a childlike way by firsthand information about the Western way of life. After the author on one of his trips to the Soviet Union had explained the creature comforts of an average middle-class home in America to a Russian friend and shown her some slides, and after she had looked at all the pictures twice, she exclaimed "If there is paradise on earth, you must live there." This comment came not from an uneducated Russian, but from a faculty member at Moscow State University.

No doubt, Russians are so fascinated by the West in part because it represents a world that in so many ways is unknown to them, a world that for the vast majority of Soviet citizens is utterly out of reach. Travel restrictions and income levels being what they are in the Soviet Union, the average citizen cannot even experience this world as a tourist. Among educated Russians one frequently encounters excessive admiration for the West. Indeed, some of them have become "internal émigrés" for all practical purposes. They have in effect become profoundly alienated from their own society.

Less educated Russians, by contrast, often display a parochial sense of Russian superiority. Most Russians are blissfully ignorant about real conditions in the West and lack firsthand knowledge about a world usually portrayed in the darkest possible colors by the Soviet press and propaganda machine.

Consequently, more than sixty years after the Revolution of 1917, Russian attitudes toward the West, in the words of one recent observer, "are a schizophrenic mixture of love and hate."[14] But it is important for us to understand that, in addition to deeply ingrained cultural factors, there are valid historical reasons for this attitude. During her long history Russia was repeatedly invaded from the West — by Sweden, Lithuania, Poland, France, and Germany. In the aftermath of the Russian Revolution foreign powers, including

the United States, intervened in the Russian Civil War in an attempt to stamp out the "menace of Bolshevism." During World
War II alone the Soviet Union lost twenty million people—a figure
equivalent to ten percent of the American population in 1970!

No wonder, then, that in the Russian mind the West constitutes a source of fear and apprehension. Twice within this century the Russian people have suffered the terrible consequences of
the application of scientific genius and modern technology on the
battlefield and have experienced war on their own soil.

Yet for a good many Russians the West has also been
associated with progress, enlightenment, refinement, and culture.
It has been an object of admiration and, for some, an object of
emulation.

The ambivalence in the Russian attitude toward the West, we
might add, has also found reflection in official Soviet thinking and
propaganda. It has consistently contrived to portray the West as a
decadent and moribund civilization, thoroughly rotten and about
to perish at any moment as the result of what is called the "general
crisis of capitalism." On the other hand, it clearly perceives the
West (and especially the United States) not only as a rival but also
as a model.

In terms of their spiritual makeup, the Russian people, as the
Russian philosopher N. Berdyaev has convincingly argued, "are an
Eastern people." "Russia is the Christian East," Berdyaev writes,
"which was for two centuries subject to the powerful influences of
the West, and whose cultured classes assimilated every Western
idea."[15] But the "Westernization" of Russia was always selective
and remained incomplete. What is more, since it proceeded in ac-
cordance with a design in which the autocracy functioned as the
chief architect, and since it was more or less forcefully imposed
from above, it called forth a powerful reaction. In the end, as Berdyaev writes, "the influences of the West . . . failed to subdue the
Russian people."[16]

The Russian Revolution of 1917 (and more particularly the
ultimate victory of the Bolsheviks) marks a distinct break in the
history of modern Russia. One of the most significant results of the
events of October 1917 was the fact that they put an end to the "St.
Petersburg period" of Russian history and in a number of ways arrested and set back the process of selective Westernization that had
been underway in Russia ever since Peter the Great.

Russia, it might be said, became re-Russified as the result of
the October Revolution. In the intellectual-cultural sphere, for example, there was an enormous setback. The upper and cultured

classes, which had been the agents or carriers of Westernization, disintegrated in the Bolshevik Revolution. In the economic sphere, too, the Westernization of Russia was arrested. The growth of the middle class and the development of capitalism were interrupted, with the New Economic Policy (1921-1927) providing only a brief and partial respite.

In the sphere of internal political development, Westernization was stopped dead in its tracks. By 1921 all political opposition was effectively decimated and dissent within the Bolshevik Party was banned. Thus, within four years after the Revolution the rudimentary and fragile structure of democratic institutions existing prior to 1917 was destroyed.

Perhaps the de-Westernization of Russia was most pronounced in the sphere of international affairs and foreign policy, the area in which Westernization in many respects had been most far-reaching and successful. After the Revolution of 1917, Russia, which in the nineteenth century had been a pillar of the European state system, dropped out of the European or Western international order.

As a matter of fact, Russia rebelled against Europe and the West. It thus contributed in a major way to the breakdown of Western political hegemony.

In short, the Russian Revolution of 1917 may be viewed as the first of a series of revolutions of a distinctly anti-Western character, representing the reaction of non-Western and underdeveloped societies to the West and the subversive influence of Westernization.

Only a few people at the time recognized the crucial significance of Russia's departure from the European state system and its rejection of the traditional system of diplomacy and international relations. Even today, many students of international affairs fail to appreciate the enormous significance of Russia's changed position in the international order, her retreat and isolation from the West, and her more or less wholesale repudiation of the Western way of life — with the important exception of science and technology.

Sir Winston Churchill was one of the few observers in the West to recognize the profound implications of the events in Russia, not only for Europe but for the whole human race. Writing in 1929 and appraising what had happened since the First World War, he called attention to the changed identity of Russia. He described it as "a state without a nation, an army without a country, a religion without a God." The Russian Revolution, he suggested, resulted in the creation of "an abyss that still continues in human affairs."[17] More than half a century has passed and, unfortunately, the "abyss in human affairs" has continued to exist to the present day. In many ways, in fact, it has become deeper.

In the Revolution of 1917, however, Russia broke with the West not only politically but also spiritually. In the name of freedom a closed society was established. That society, moreover, in the name of a supposedly stateless future social order, came to be dominated by the most colossal state on earth. N. Bukharin, who soon was to become one of its victims, called it "a gigantic machine the like of which mankind has not seen in any era of its existence."[18]

In the aftermath of 1917 a socialist restoration of autocracy took place in Russia, a restoration of a style of political rule that — though not identical in every respect to the traditional autocracy — meant in essence a reversion to a four-century-old pattern of political rule. This was the very thing G. V. Plekhanov, Lenin's erstwhile teacher, had warned against as early as the 1880s. Such a restoration reached its culmination in the long reign of Stalin. He not only reestablished an extreme version of autocratic rule but also reintroduced serfdom in the form of forced collectivization in the 1930s.

An examination of the political posture of the Soviet Union after 1917 reveals a number of distinct and important characteristics: (1) the establishment of a single power center; (2) an intense preoccupation with the building of a strong, centralized state; (3) a deliberate and active policy of territorial expansion, aimed in this case at reestablishing control over all territories that had formerly been part of the Russian Empire; and (4) an official attitude of intense hostility toward the West.

If we project this political posture against the background of Russian history, we find that it coincides most closely with the political stance of Muscovite Russia, i.e., the Russia that had "gathered the Russian lands," setting into motion the process of territorial aggrandizement that resulted in the expansion of the original principality of Moscow. This principality, which consisted of a few thousand square miles, was exploded into a huge empire occupying one-fifth of the earth's surface.

The "gathering of Russian lands," this unparalleled process of territorial expansion, was achieved at the cost of subordinating the interests of the individual and even entire social classes to the state. Summarizing modern Russian history from the sixteenth to the midnineteenth century, the most distinguished prerevolutionary

Russian historian, V. O. Kliuchevsky, wrote ". . . the expansion of state territory, which strained beyond measure and exhausted the resources of the people, only increased the power of the state without elevating the selfconsciousness of the people. . . . The state swelled up, the people grew lean."[19]

As a recent essay by Robert C. Tucker has made clear, the pattern of "state building" and the traditional state domination of society in Russia has continued into the present.[20] Russian society has not yet succeeded in emancipating itself from the domination of the state. On the contrary, the power of the state in the Soviet era is not only undivided but is also far more extensive, not to say all-embracing.[21] Indeed, today the Soviet Union stands as a giant monument to one of the great illusions of our age: the illusion of the transitoriness of total power.

Whether one examines the cultural, religious, economic, or more narrowly political aspects of Russian life, one finds that the state played an enormous role in the development of Russia even before 1917. This role was much more prominent than that played by the state in Western Europe or in the United States. In fact, the state loomed so large in Russian life that this particular aspect of the nation's experience gave rise to a theory, argued by the so-called state school of Russian historiography, according to which the state was the chief agent and moving force in Russian history. In this perspective on the Russian past, the Russian state, unlike its counterpart in Western Europe, was viewed not as the product but as the creator of social classes.

It comes as no surprise that this interpretation of the role of the state in Russian history gave rise to the hopeful, if incongruous, idea of enlightened despotism or progressive autocracy. The idea of "a revolutionary on the throne of Russia" did not escape the attention of Russian revolutionaries in the nineteenth and twentieth centuries, including Trotsky and Lenin, who came to look upon the state both as the chief target and as an important and essential instrument of the revolution.[22]

The original goals of the Bolshevik Revolution notwithstanding, it is important to recognize that the Soviet Union, as a result of the restoration of socialist autocracy under Stalin, has become a polity in which the process of state building has continued virtually unabated. As in the past, this process is wedded primarily to military objectives, with all the attendant consequences for the citizens of the Soviet Union and everyone else. While this circumstance, without a doubt, is in part a response to the threat the West has posed and continues to pose to the Soviet Union, we should be aware that the pursuit of military power (formerly for regional, now for global objectives) has been a matter of long-standing tradition in Russia. It is, moreover, dictated by Marxist-Leninist ideology, which perceives the world in terms of light and darkness and regards conflict between classes and among nations as natural, normal, and inherent in the human condition prior to the advent of the Communist millennium.

It is also important to recognize the fact that Communism resolves the classic conflict between the individual and society unequivocally in favor of society. It does so, in fact, to the point of completely crushing the individual if necessary (and frequently even when no reasonable definition of *raison d'état* would explain, let alone justify, such action). It is no accident that in recent years there has been a wave of defections, a veritable exodus of prominent cultural figures from the Soviet Union, people who enjoyed all the privileges and advantages that high social status in the Soviet Union entails.

As Christians we should also be aware that the Soviet Union represents an extreme—and perhaps *the* extreme!—of a culturally regimented society in modern times. It is a society in which the expression of dissent in any form is treated as a grave crime against the state, a society in which religious believers, from Russian Orthodox Christians to Moslems, are subjected to persistent and systematic persecution.[23]

As Christians we should also realize that when we interact with the Soviet Union—especially through the medium of organized exchanges, group visits, international conferences and exhibits, etc.—we are dealing with "an ideology in power," an ideology that denies individuality as well as God and has raised a nonexisting mythical social collectivity to the status of a new and omnipotent divinity.

In the name of this divinity, countless lives have been destroyed, families separated, traditions ruthlessly brushed aside, and history falsified beyond all recognition. To advance the cause of this mythical collectivity, creativity has been stifled, regimented, and suppressed. An officially approved style of artistic expression, which goes under the name of "socialist realism," has been imposed and enforced. Artists whose work does not conform to the canons of socialist realism have had their paintings and sculptures bulldozed into oblivion—on the orders of a government whose constitution, among other things, guarantees freedom of expression.

Within the past twenty-five years, Russia has produced three Nobel Prize laureates in literature. Boris Pasternak (1958) was forced by the Soviet government to reject the award. A. I. Solzhenitsyn (1970) was forcefully expelled from his native land amidst a government-orchestrated campaign of vilification. The work of both of these writers is still not fully and freely available to the reading public in the Soviet Union. Only M. Sholokhov (1965), whose work falls within the parameters of socialist realism, is among the approved writers whose work is published in the Soviet Union.

Finally, Christians first and foremost should be aware of the full extent of the difficulty (and danger) involved in seeking reconciliation with the Soviet Union. Let us recall Tiutchev's exhortation, cited at the outset, that Russia "cannot be measured with an ordinary yardstick." The unfortunate and tragic fact is that the Soviet Union, i.e., modern Russia, is not a conventional state. Communism is not merely another political or social philosophy. In addition to all the attributes of a modern nation state, the Soviet Union also represents a messianic force in human affairs. It constitutes an incipient, embryonic new world order. The reason for the passionate antireligious propaganda and zealous persecution of religion and any form of dissent must be sought in the fact that Communism itself is a kind of religion, a secular faith that in the final analysis cannot tolerate any other competing faith or creed.

In short, we are dealing with a pseudotheocratic type of polity. It is a polity that allows no distinction between state, society, and church; it is a polity that reduces the individual to a function of the collective; it is a polity that seeks nothing less than the complete reconstruction of the world and perceives in the very existence of other non-Communist, or even independent Communist, states the negation of its own identity and purpose.

"Russian communism," Berdyaev writes, "is a communism of the East."[24] We can ignore this fact only at our own peril. Berdyaev's observation, among other things, calls our attention to the fact that Soviet Communism is the descendant of Leninism, i.e., Eastern-oriented Marxism. It is a political doctrine that in the course of its development has found itself increasingly at variance with Western Marxism. It is a doctrine in which the idea of socialism in the end has become irrevocably divorced from the idea of democracy and become fused instead with Russian nationalism.

The "Eastern orientation" of Leninism has, among other things, led to the development of a distinctively new theory of world revolution. This theory is Eastern-oriented and different from classical Marxism in that it centers around the idea of the potentially revolutionary character of the peasantry. It is a theory according to which world revolution and socialism could develop in one country and, in contrast to what Marx had maintained, in an economically backward and underdeveloped country. Moreover, it is a theory that envisages a direct transition to socialism, bypassing the liberal, bourgeois-capitalist stage of economic development, which Plekhanov regarded as being so essential in the case of Russia. It is a theory, finally, that looks upon the colonies as an anti-imperialist force that will cooperate with the proletariat in a united front against imperialism.

The "Eastern orientation" of Russian Communism has been most forcefully expressed by Stalin, who as early as 1906 had visions of the "Russian proletariat . . . marching at the head of the democratic revolution."[25] In November 1918, only a year after the Bolshevik seizure of power, Stalin spoke of the "worldwide significance of the October Revolution" and pointed out that it was not only the first revolution in history to awaken the colonial East from its age-long sleep, but also a "living, salvation-bringing example" to the West.[26] A month later he expressed his conviction that the revolutionary movement in the East would ignite a revolution in the West and spoke of Soviet Russia as the "standard-bearer of the world revolution."[27]

For our purposes it is important to recognize, first of all, that Lenin transformed the Europe-centered and Western-oriented doctrine of Marxism into Leninism or Bolshevism, i.e., a doctrine of world revolution in which the pivotal role was played by the East and, more particularly, by Russia.

Second, we must be aware that Lenin telescoped the Marxian idea of class conflict into a life and death struggle between East and West. In other words, in Leninism the issue of capitalism versus Communism or socialism assumed the character and dimensions of an East-West struggle. In his last published article, Lenin explained that this struggle was between "the counterrevolutionary imperialist West and the revolutionary and nationalist East, between the most civilized countries of the world and the Orientally-backward countries."[28]

Thus, the revolutionary movement of which Soviet Russia came to be the nucleus, in its ultimate political impact, proved to be directed against the West. In Lenin's mind there was never any doubt as to the outcome of the East-West struggle. "In the final analysis," he wrote in the last year of his life, "the outcome of the struggle will be determined by the fact that Russia, India, China, etc., constitute the overwhelming majority of the population. . . . In this sense, the ultimate victory of socialism is completely and absolutely assured."[29] In other words, Lenin envisaged a coalition of Russia, China, India, and other Third World countries against the West. If the United States today finds itself at loggerheads with Russia in Europe and in the Third World, it is because of many factors, including the past, present, and likely future conduct of the United States in world affairs. But *one* reason has to do with the fact that the confrontation is unequivocally dictated by the postulates of Leninism, i.e., the doctrine that has become the official creed of the Soviet Union.

In emphasizing the fundamental differences between the United States (or the West) and Russia, the intent of this chapter has not been to argue against a reconciliation between East and West. It has, rather, been to suggest something about the enormous difficulties that, in my view, are involved in such an endeavor.

If we are truly serious about building bridges to the other side, common sense and prudence dictate that we should calculate rather precisely the distances we need to span, and that we should know something about the topography, soil structure, and climate of the land on the other side. The best and most noble intentions, while laudable and necessary, are not sufficient for this task.

In the nuclear age, it seems to me, neither superpower has a realistic alternative to reconciliation. Furthermore, as Christians, I believe, we have no choice but to seek reconciliation. The commandment "Love thine enemy" or, as I prefer, "Love thy neighbor" is categorical and, presumably, all-inclusive!

But in seeking reconciliation with the Russians, on both a personal and an official level, our expectations as to the possibilities and likely results should be tempered by a realization of the magnitude of the task. To this end we should make use of every opportunity for person-to-person contacts, every chance we have to learn more about the Russians, their history, culture and civilization, their hopes and disappointments, their successes, problems and failures, their dreams and aspirations, and their everyday life. And we should also afford them every possible opportunity to learn more about us, to form a more accurate and realistic picture of the West, which for many Russians still remains—in the language of Alexander Herzen—"the other shore" they would very much like to visit.

2

ARE THEY ATHEISTS OR BELIEVERS?: THE RUSSIAN SOUL

Paul Vallière

To ask of any historic people in modern times "Are they atheists or believers?" is on the face of it to ask a simplistic question. There are so many critical distinctions the question glides over that one wonders how meaningful any answer could be.

There is the distinction between personal religious faith and identification with a historic religious tradition. Which are we asking about? What is the relation between them?

There is the complexity and pluralism of modern society. Can the spiritual quest of any people in modern times be reduced to a simple either / or question?

Then there is the difficulty of interpreting what people say they believe. Opinion polls in the United States consistently show that a large majority of Americans say they believe in God. But what does this fact mean? What does it tell us about American church life, social life, or concepts of God? Obviously we cannot say without knowing more about many other things.

Finally, we must remember that in the Soviet Union direct and open surveys of public opinion are not allowed, statistics on religious belief and affiliation are not published, and studies that treat religion with a measure of objectivity are rare.

Thus, generalizations about contemporary Russian belief must be treated as educated guesses. Much of the evidence has to be drawn indirectly from literature, film, the newspapers, interviews with émigrés, and limited opportunities for personal observation.

Yet, in spite of its problems and the impossibility of answering it definitively, "Are the Russians atheists or believers?" remains an important question. It is important first of all because the Russians themselves would recognize it as such. For the Russians the question of atheism or belief is a practical as well as a theoretical question, an issue of everyday life. This is because the Soviet Union, where most Russians live, is an ideological state, and atheism is an essential part of the ideology. Thus, the expression of religious belief, while tolerated within certain narrow limits, necessarily situates persons and groups in an antagonistic relationship to one of the founding principles of their social and political system. The antagonism may never be openly expressed, but it is always felt. It has to be felt in a country where atheism is not and cannot be confined to the realm of personal conscience, in a system which demands that atheism be public, always vocal, always a missionary atheism. "Are the Russians atheists or believers?" is a question that interrogates the Soviet system at one of its roots.

The question of atheism or belief also bears on the historical self-understanding of the Russian people, specifically on the important issue of how being "Russian" is related to being "Soviet." The two are not the same. The Soviet value system is based on an internationalist ideology with spiritual and intellectual roots that are completely Western. A powerful synthesis of English political economy, German philosophy, and French revolutionary practice, Marxism was already a fully developed value system by the time it first came to Russia in the 1880s and 1890s. It was not much more Russian by the time it seized power in Russia in 1917. Lenin, Trotsky, and their colleagues violently rejected traditional Russian values and institutions. Their aim was to internationalize Russia, not to Russianize Marxism. The historic institutions that gave content to being Russian beyond the accidents of race and language were either swept away or drastically marginalized by the Revolution.

These included the monarchy, the Orthodox Church, and traditional rural society. With these institutions set aside and an internationalist ideology put in their place, what did it mean to be Russian? The religious dimension of this question was especially conspicuous. The institutions of old Russia were grounded in some way in Orthodoxy, whereas those of the young Soviet state were founded on atheism.

To Western eyes everything that happens in Russia naturally tends to appear Russian. Because the Soviet state grew up in Russia, it too has seemed to be as Russian as it is Soviet. In recent years there has been a growing awareness of the importance of the non-Russian peoples in the Soviet Union. Yet even this discovery often tends to reinforce the identification of "Russian" and "Soviet" in Western minds. Because the leaders of the Soviet Union are for the most part ethnic Russians and because the Russian language plays a leading role in the Soviet state system, it is often assumed that the Russians must be practicing a kind of ethnic imperialism: Russians rule non-Russian peoples in the name of Soviet ideology but in fact serve Russian national interests.

The trouble with this assumption is that it ignores the many areas of life, such as religion, where historic Russian tradition and Soviet Marxist ideology are in deep conflict with other. This conflict is one of the most important factors governing Russian life in the Soviet Union today.

Of course, there would be no conflict if in the sixty-seven years since the Revolution most Russians had become atheists. But this has not happened. The main result of decades of atheist preaching and administrative oppression of religion seems to be a lazy indifference to religion in many segments of the population. It coexists with continuing, often fervent, religious belief among a large minority. Westerners, including Western Christians, sometimes make the mistake of seeing religious indifference as evidence of the success of atheistic preaching. Is there much difference, after all, between apathy toward religion and atheism? The two tend to blend together in the West.

We must remember, however, that the Soviet system is not founded on the principle of indifference to religion but on the falsity of religion and the "scientific" truth of an atheistic view of the world. Atheism is embodied in all levels of the school curriculum, in the press and the electronic media, and in most popular scientific and cultural activities. The fact that all this effort produces not atheism but something else represents a failure of the ideology to win acceptance for its "scientific" claims. In an ideological system such a failure is a grave matter, for an ideology always presents itself as an interconnected whole. If a significant part of the whole turns out to be dubious, the entire system may be thrown into doubt.

To make matters worse (from the Soviet point of view), the failure of atheism is accompanied by the continuing vitality of religion. The outward practice of atheism in the Soviet Union, because it is compulsory in many situations, is almost certainly more widespread than atheistic belief. The opposite is true in the case of religion. Although rejected by the Soviet establishment and subject to severe limitations on expression, religious belief is almost certainly much more widespread than the public practice of religion would suggest.

Furthermore, the public practice of religion is by no means insignificant. It has to confine itself to services of worship. Churches are not permitted to conduct formal religious education or to engage in any kind of public evangelism, social service, or political advocacy. Nevertheless, the full churches and the fervor of the services of all denominations provide ample evidence of the vitality of religion.

It is also important to keep in mind that the churches are by far the largest independent organizations in the Soviet Union—independent in the sense of not sponsored by or supported by the government or the Party. By a conservative estimate the membership of the Russian Orthodox Church stands at about forty million people. The Communist Party of the Soviet Union has about eighteen million members.[1] In fairness to the Party we must remember that membership is carefully controlled and subject to periodic purges, whereas membership in the Russian Orthodox Church is looser. Still, membership in the church is also completely voluntary, a fact that, when combined with the number of people involved, makes the church a weighty institution in the Soviet Union today.

The Russian Orthodox Church is not the only church with adherents among the Russians. Protestantism, mainly represented by Baptist and Pentecostal churches, is lively presence on the Russian scene, especially in the cities, and it may be expected to grow in the decades ahead. Judaism, too, will continue to exist in Russia, although its numbers are in decline because of emigration and its institutions are subject to the most severe administrative oppression.

We must also remember that not all members of the Russian Orthodox Church are Russians. A large number are Ukrainians and Byelorussians, especially from those parts of the Ukraine and Byelorussia permanently incorporated into the Soviet Union only after World War II. The Orthodox churches in these areas escaped the worst Soviet persecutions of religion, which took place in the 1920s and 1930s. They are somewhat stronger institutionally than the Orthodox churches in many other parts of the country. Orthodoxy is also the predominant faith among the Georgians, the Moldavians, and some smaller minorities. (An ancient and important doctrinal difference that will not soon be healed separates the Armenian Church from the Orthodox Church. The Russian Old Believers, who split off from the state church in the seventeenth century, are separated from the Russian Orthodox by less significant differences, so reunion is not impossible.)

Still, in spite of the religious pluralism of the Russian people, Russian Orthodoxy has a centrality on the Russian religious scene that no other church or even all the other churches combined cannot match. There are two reasons for this beyond the mere numerical predominance of Orthodoxy: the intellectual tradition of Russian Orthodoxy and the significance of Orthodoxy as a link with the Russian past.

The intellectual tradition is a rich legacy that has scarcely begun to be spent. Even without the Russian contribution Orthodoxy already contained a powerful intellectual inheritance from Greek Christianity. Then, starting in the nineteenth century, the Russians enriched this tradition by creating a highly original modern literature, philosophy and theology—the first Eastern Orthodox people in modern times to do so. This accomplishment gave—and still gives—the Russians a special role to play in the intellectual life of Orthodox Christianity in the modern world. It also gives modern Russian intellectuals a solid foundation on which to reconstruct a spiritual tradition when one is needed—and one is needed every time an individual or group of Russians comes to recognize the emptiness of contemporary Soviet atheism. Dostoyevsky, Tolstoy, Soloviev, Berdyaev—these are the sources to which Russian intellectuals first turn when the official sources, Marx and Lenin, run dry.

The force of this point must not be trivialized by making modern Russia out to be a place where large numbers of ex-atheist intellectuals are being converted to a spiritual consensus based on the Christian ideals of Dostoyevsky or Tolstoy. The Soviet Union comprises a dynamic modern society in which many different groups of people are exploring innumerable conflicting spiritual options simultaneously. Even among avowed Russian Orthodox intellectuals there is not a consensus on such questions as church reform, the role of Orthodoxy in Soviet society, the relation of Orthodoxy to Russian nationalism, the reform of the Soviet system, the prospects of democracy in Russia, or the relation of Russia to the West.

Furthermore, while Russian intellectuals today cannot ignore their country's Orthodox heritage, they do not necessarily feel bound to it. Almost seven decades of iconoclasm and modernization have had an enormous impact on the way friend and foe alike perceive Orthodoxy.

Yet the development of modern Soviet society also affects atheism. Indeed, it is an open question at present whether modern trends are disrupting atheism or religion more. After all, why should any contemporary Russian intellectuals, not to speak of believers, limit themselves to an atheist framework when there are so many other interesting paths to explore? This would be the case even if Soviet atheism were in the best of health—which it is clearly not. In addition to being compromised by its status as official dogma, it seems to have run out of ideas and cogent expositors. Russian intellectuals will often tell the Western inquirer that if it is atheism he is looking for, he had better look at home in Paris or New York where atheism is at least philosophically interesting, but surely not in Moscow.

The Orthodox Church is also one of the main links with the Russian past in the contemporary Soviet Union. Much diminished as an institution and still sorely oppressed, the church nevertheless exists. The monarchy, on the other hand, is gone forever. Russian rural society, ruined by the collectivization programs of the 1920s and 1930s, will have to be rebuilt from the ground up along different lines from those of the old Russian village.

Furthermore, the church not only exists but promises to grow in strength in the decades ahead. Administrative oppression has kept the size and scope of the Orthodox Church at artifically low levels. The demand for clergy, church buildings, and religious education of all kinds far exceeds the supply. Thus, any significant liberalization of controls on the church is almost sure to open the way to a dramatic resurgence of the institution—which is one of the main reasons why the Soviet state is reluctant to relax its grip.

To say that the church provides a link with the Russian past is not to suggest that her value to contemporary Russians is that of a museum of culture or a focal point for nostalgia. Love of the past is an understandable and laudable phenomenon in a society founded on an ideology as present-minded as Marxism.

Still, the reason why Russians today are exploring links with their past has to do not just with love of the past but with the state of affairs in the present. The fact is that the Soviet system is not functioning very well in many sectors. The industrial economy is sluggish, the working class demoralized, the rural economy in a shambles, the natural environment polluted, bribery rife, alcoholism more rampant than ever. Also, these shortcomings are more pronounced in much of the central and northern heartland of Russia than in many of the non-Russian regions of the Soviet Union.

It is natural, therefore, that thoughtful Russians of all persuasions should be inquiring into ways of improving things. Their inquiry has to begin with a reevaluation of the guiding assumptions of the Soviet era, such as the assumption that the road to a better future demanded a complete break with the past. The Revolution condemned Old Russia—tsarist, Orthodox, and rural—as a realm of darkness. The leaders awaited a Soviet Russia — socialist, atheistic, and industrial — as a realm of light and truth.

Almost seven decades later such a future still appears remote. Could it be that Russia made too sharp a break with its past, that it impaired the future because it discarded its foundation in the past? If so, does it not follow that those who would reform the present should give careful attention to links with the past that still exist in Russia and seek ways of turning them to good account for the Russia of tomorrow?

Contemporary Russian literature, journalism, and film, not just in dissident circles but in established quarters, too, recognizes the need for a greater appreciation of Russian tradition. A couple of examples drawn from recent Soviet Russian fiction (not dissident) will serve to illustrate the point. In both cases the authors make use of a favorite symbolic representation of tradition in Russian literature: an old grandmother, ailing yet enduring. In her fidelity to the past and her physical and spiritual endurance she represents the passive resistance of tradition to modernity, of historic Russia to the Soviet present.

The first example comes from a story by Fyodor Abramov, "Wooden Horses" (1969). The setting is a modest household in a northern village. The paternal grandmother visits her family. Though she is a native of the locality, she now lives in town with other members of her family. Her visit provides an occasion for reviewing her life story, which more or less recapitulates the catastrophes of the Russian national tradition in modern times. First, it was male tyranny in an unreformed, violent northern village. Next, the destruction of the germ of productive and civilized rural life by forced collectivization. The loss of sons in the war and a daughter to the moral laxity of the postwar years followed. Finally, she bore the ignominy of dependence on her youngest son, Ivan, an irresponsible drunkard cut off from the native soil. Milentievna, as she is called, bears the experiences patiently through the strength of her character and a firm, Orthodox sense of identity.

At the end of the story she is waiting for her son Ivan to fetch her back to town. She has promised her granddaughter to accompany her back to school — a detail Abramov perhaps wants us to take as a ray of hope for the future of tradition. But the good-for-nothing Ivan does not show up. The old lady is forced to hitch a ride back to town in a passing truck. This sets up the closing picture of Milentievna:

> The vehicle stopped. Unfortunately there was no room in the cab with the driver, for his pale wife with a newborn baby in

her arms already sat there. But Milentievna did not give a moment's thought to whether or not she would ride in the back.

The back of the truck was huge, with high forged sides, and she disappeared into it as if down a well. But for a long time beneath the dark vault of spruce forest densely encircling the road I could make out a bobbing white spot.

It was Milentievna bouncing with the truck over potholes and ruts, waving farewell to me with her kerchief.[2]

The picture is a commentary on the situation of tradition in the modern world. There is no room for the longsuffering mother in the cab as it lurches along a bad road to the world of the future. Yet the old mother is not left behind altogether. She sits facing backwards, waving farewell as she speeds out of the past, her white kerchief a comforting point of orientation for the beholder.

The second example comes from a novel by Valentin Rasputin, *Farewell to Matyora* (1979). The novel depicts the last few months of a village located on an island in the Angara River in Siberia. A new hydroelectric facility is about to wipe the island, Matyora, out. The only inhabitants remaining on Matyora as the story begins are old people, some children in their care, and two or three misfits. The focus is on a group of old women who are wont to gather in the cottage of an ancient widow named Darya. There they are frequently joined by a queer old male tramp named Bogodul, who lives in a broken-down barracks on Matyora. The women's chief topic of conversation is the imminent doom of Matyora and with it the end of the only way of life they have ever known. Each step in the closing down of the island wrenches their feelings — the evacuation and incineration of the cottages, the felling of the timber, the removal of the domestic animals and harvested crops.

At one point early in the narrative old Bogodul (whose name means "God's servant") bursts into Darya's cottage with the evil tidings that unidentified outsiders have appeared in the village cemetery and are busy uprooting and burning gravemarkers and crosses. These "devils," as he calls them, in fact are merely a sanitation crew from a public health station that has orders from the authorities to complete the cleansing of the island. Led by Darya, the ancient company rushes to the scene in protest:

The cemetery lay beyond the village on the road to the mill, on a dry sandy knoll among birches and pines, and you could see far along the Angara and its shores from there. First, leaning forward and stretching her arms as though picking berries, came Darya with firmly set lips, which betrayed her toothless mouth; Natasya barely managed to keep up: she suffered from shortness of breath, and gasping, she bobbed her head frequently. Behind

them, holding the boy by hand, minced Sima. Bogodul fell
behind to arouse the village, and the old women flew into the
cemetery alone.

They were finishing up their work there, putting the downed
headstones, beds, and crosses into a pile to make a bonfire. A
huge bearlike man in a green waterproof jacket and matching
pants, trampling the graves, was carrying the ancient wooden
grave markers in his arms when Darya, using the last of her
energy to surge ahead, hit his arm with a stick she had picked up.
The blow was weak, but the shock made the man drop his
burden on the ground and exclaim: "What's the matter, what is
it, old woman?"

"Hup, now march out of here, you evil spirit!" Darya
shouted, choking on fear and rage, and brandished the stick
once more. The man jumped back.[3]

The scene protests the desecration not just of a particular
cemetery but of tradition as such. The cemetery at Matyora
represents, as it were, the accumulated witness of generations of
Orthodox Christian villagers that is threatened with obliteration in
the name of public health and the modernization of the region—in
the name of "progress." The enemy is identified: not just the
workmen but their bosses, the distant officialdom giving orders
without regard to the individuals affected or their collective sense
of values, their reverence for a sacred tradition.

Like "Wooden Horses," *Farewell to Matyora* ends with a picture in which a longsuffering grandmother and a motor vehicle are
juxtaposed. At the end of the tale Darya, a couple of her friends,
and Bogodul are the only human beings left on Matyora. They were
supposed to have been evacuated already, but there has been a
delay. The official charged with the evacuation has just discovered
the delay and is mortified, for a party of government inspectors is
to arrive the next morning. They expect to find the job of cleaning
out Matyora finished. The official and a couple of companions, including Darya's son, set out by motor boat in the middle of an
unusually foggy night to make their way to Matyora to pick up the
stragglers. But they cannot see where they are going, lose their way,
and aimlessly cruise about in the currents of the Angara. On the
island Darya and her companions huddle in her cottage, frightened
by the dark night and thick fog. The wind picks up, and in the
distance the muffled sound of a motor can just barely be heard.

Once again we have an arresting commentary on a modern
society in which the link with tradition has become problematic.
The authentic bearers of tradition huddle in obscurity on the edge
of society, while those in charge, short on gasoline yet unable to

find their destination, drive the vehicle of modernity around in circles.

"Are they atheists or believers?" The question remains interesting, even though no simple answer can be given. The Russian people today face a modern world as complex and pluralistic as our own. No single religious system, and certainly no one ideology, can possibly embrace all of it and solve all of its problems. Every important reform will have to be nourished from many sources. But one thing may be predicted: whenever and wherever the day of reform dawns in the Soviet system, religion will be a part of it — indeed, in the middle of it. The need for roots in a tradition and the intellectual excitement of religion for a people oppressed by stale atheism, not to speak of the God who makes all things new, will keep religion very much alive in Soviet Russia for a long time to come.

3

WHAT ARE THE PEOPLE REALLY LIKE?

The Face of the Russian Church

Anthony Ugolnik

Twin anecdotes reveal how much of a mystery American and Russian Christians remain to one another. Of Russian ethnic background, married to a Greek American, I worship with my family at the only Eastern Orthodox Church in our mid-American town. A prominent sign marks the predominantly Greek parish as the "Hellenic Orthodox Church." One of my neighbors, once he got to know me well, made a sheepish admission.

"Once I thought you might be a devil worshipper," he said, looking away from me in embarrassment as I laughed in surprise.

"A *devil* worshiper? Whatever gave you that crazy idea?" I knew people were generally ignorant of our faith and often treated us as if we were members of some strange sect, but never had I heard this characterization of our worship.

"Well, you know . . . the sign says *Hell*enic Church, and you being Russian and all . . . ." He too laughed, with the relief of one who recognizes his own foolishness.

The next year, when I first worshiped at a Moscow church when I was in the Soviet Union, I remembered that incident when I struck up a conversation with a pious Russian woman, a schoolteacher from the provinces, accompanied by her twelve-year-old son. We drank in each other's lives eagerly, with the thirst of fellow Orthodox separated widely now by space and culture. She told me of her home parish and the wide loyalty it commanded in her town. She shared with me her concern about her son, now old enough to face pressure against belief that state-sponsored social organizations fostered. Yet she radiated a pride in her church and clearly measured me against the Christian standard set here in her "Orthodox homeland."

"Tell me something," she asked after we had exchanged our names and a customary promise to commend each other in prayer. She seemed reluctant to come forth with her question. "Is it true," she asked through squinted eyes. "I have read. . . . do they have Satan worshipers in your country, and temples to the devil?"

Strange though this absolutely spontaneous parallel seems, it belies the distance between Eastern and Western Christians. Though theologians are beginning to fathom spaces between us, the average Christian tends to commit his counterpart, East or West, to a hell of one kind or another. Even now, when thousands of Orthodox churches of various ethnic origins raise their domes in American towns and cities, and hundreds of thousands of Americans worship in them, we too often remain a mystery to each other. In that ignorance we waste a precious resource, for in Orthodox Christianity any American believer can listen to the heartbeat of Christian Russia.

One of the privileges of my life has been to come to know the Soviet people well. I have come to appreciate them, believers and nonbelievers alike, as fellow human beings. I have shared a feeling with many Orthodox Christians who have had the opportunity to come to know the Soviet Union. Perhaps because we dwell spiritually in a tradition so little known to our fellow Americans, we feel at home and religiously at ease in the land our media constantly portray as "atheistic."

Though some Orthodox of Russian background routinely travel to the Soviet Union on religiously oriented tours, I have gone there individually for research and as the teacher-escort for American student groups studying Soviet art and literature. Thus, in Moscow and Leningrad, Kiev and Kishinev, Odessa and Zagorsk I have passed as a Russian Christian, taken the sacraments in their churches, and shared regular fellowship with believers. I speak Russian, but I have never been a part of any official religious "delegation." My friendships have been with laypeople in the Russian church, whom I see unescorted. I know a few Catholics in the Soviet Union, but I have never met any of the Baptist or evangelical minority.

Despite sporadic media attention to the problems of Christianity in Russia, I am troubled that Americans know so little of Russian Christians. It is not right that our brothers and sisters in the Soviet Union should be faceless. They deserve to have us see, briefly, a small slice of their spirit.

The church is everywhere in the Soviet Union. Let me assure you that Christianity, especially in its Orthodox form, is pervasive in Russia. Many Russians identify themselves quite frankly as "believers," a term much more frequent than "Christian." They pray. If a working church is within commuting distance, they worship openly. If there is no church close by, they go to great trouble to find one.

Westerners can be blind to the Spirit in Russia because they do not recognize his Orthodox form. Believers and nonbelievers are not quite so incessantly polarized as we might suspect. The Russian grandmother babysitting in the park is likely to be a Christian and to teach her grandchildren the sign of the cross and basic prayers before they ever learn the official atheist line. Families often split along theological lines — a brother is a believer, an aunt belongs to the Party, a grandmother is piously observant (all too many of the grandfathers died in the war), yet a daughter is ignorant of religious matters but believes, somehow, in a God.

Lenin is as omnipresent an image in Russia as are the well-fed, dazzle-smiled models who symbolize the good life in U.S. advertising. Any of these images can stand in the way of the gospel, but none of them can kill it. Our Christian social movement in the United States has been shaped in reaction to the consumer culture. Under socialism, surrounded by idealized images of the worker, burdened by antireligious legislation, the Spirit in Russia has taken on his own subtle shades that can instruct us as we discern them.

Clearly, the ministry of the church in Russia is very different from our own, at least in its emphasis. Christians take contradiction totally for granted. Pecherskaya Lavra, the Monastery of the Caves in Kiev famous among Orthodox as the cradle of Russian Christendom, is now a museum complex. At the entrance to the caverns where the hallowed monks are buried, guides assemble the groups they will lead through the caves.

I watched a Russian group from Leningrad. They nodded agreeably as the guide recited, in a bored monotone, the "superstitions" of the monks and the supposed miracle that preserved the bodies in the dry, natural embalming that the caves provided. Some even took notes.

Out of curiosity, and with some Orthodox outrage at the tone of the guide and the simplistic antireligious slogans on the walls, I tagged onto the end of the single-file procession through the narrow, twisting caves. I was not prepared for what I saw. The guide, far ahead, was well out of sight. The Russians at the end of the line crossed themselves. Many bowed, as is our custom, before the relics. Some left petitions for prayer scratched on shreds of paper, stuffing them into the icon-studded niches in the walls. And these were the same people who nodded so agreeably to the guide. Their resistance takes a different form, you see, from our own.

Christians in Russia begin by taking the last place at the banquet. Western visitors to Russia often conclude that the churches are filled with the old and uneducated. Seldom do they discover, unless they worship and converse with believers, that Christians dress like and have the demeanor of the old and the rejected. Believers in Russia "dress down" for church, in direct contradiction of our own custom.

Christianity in Russia is incompatible with success. Those who desire the Soviet equivalent of rising the corporate ladder can hardly speed that rise with membership at the right parish. To become a regular worshiper is to choose the way of Christ over the way of the world. As the psalm goes, chanted at the beginning of every Orthodox liturgy in Russia, "Put not your trust in princes, in sons of men, in whom there is no salvation" (Psalm 146:3).

Following that psalm, the Russian choir intones the beatitudes, which draw the congregation into their spell. They are the laws of the kingdom proclaimed in the liturgy, and they embody the spirituality of the Russian church. It is hard to convey the joyous spirit, the almost palpable faith at the monastery in Zagorsk as the masses of pilgrims join the choir in singing "Blessed are you when men shall revile you, and persecute you, and say all manner of evil against you falsely, for my sake, for great is you reward in heaven."

I feel God's presence nowhere so strongly as I do in Russia. The Soviet posters proclaim the worker triumphant over the material conditions of his being. The Soviet church has incorporated some of the same consciousness and, in the grand ideological transformation (or subversion) typical of our faith, the church has transfigured it. Christ the worker, Christ the peasant, Christ the fool triumphs over the powerful, the rich, and the wise.

Christians in Russia focus upon the self-emptying of God, the divine condescension of Christ in becoming human, as their spiritual model. Mary, the *Bogoroditsa,* "Birth-giver of God," is a manifestation of God immanent in the humble.

Yuri is a solemn young engineering student in Leningrad. He scowls when he walks, as do many Russians — you've met these faces in our media portraits of Soviets. Daily, you will find him with that same round, Slavic face rapt in prayer before an icon of the Mother of God in one of Leningrad's churches.

Yuri had only a copy of the Gospels, not in modern Russian but in the liturgical language of Old Church Slavonic, which he studied to better understand the Word. Given a Bible as a gift, he scanned the modern Russian text through tears of gratitude. (Those scowling Russians can be intensely emotional.)

In serious conversation he professes to prefer his own dilemma to ours. "It is difficult for us, especially in the outreaches like Siberia and Central Asia. No Bibles, no churches — but we survive. With us, the choices are plain. But from what I know of you, the choices seem insidious. Materialism among us is an ideology. We can combat it. But with you, it seems to me, materialism is a hidden presumption. Your battle is the harder to fight." If you pray for Yuri in his struggle, remember also that he prays for you.

Yuri's choices, however difficult, have not involved him in radically open declarations of faith. I first saw Olga at vespers services in a central Russian city. Her dress drew my attention. Though it is common for young believers to dress simply — babushkas or shawls for the women and nondescript, coarse dark coats for the men — Olga was dressed in a modified nun's habit with a long dark dress and a veil pinned beneath her chin. She clutched in her hand a long black staff. Crossing herself, bowing deeply through the long litanies of the evening service, she was known to the other worshipers and frequently interrupted her devotions with a smile to one, or a few kisses, Russian style, to another.

Olga is a "nun in the world." With opportunities to enter the monastic life severely limited, this becomes an option in Soviet Russia. Although she was educated for a clerical profession, her radical choice to be so open a believer has committed her to another way of life. She is content in a menial job, that of a street sweeper, which occupies her early morning hours. She is able, then, to attend the daily liturgies that take place in most Orthodox churches in the Soviet Union. Though she punctuates her conversation with signs of the cross and expressions of faith, she is a product of modern Soviet education. She has willingly taken upon herself the contemporary equivalent of an ancient Russian choice: to become a "fool for Christ," a poor person, a pilgrim who gives to others her testimony to the fullness of the Spirit.

These younger believers exist in increasing numbers. Many of them are, in a sense, converts to the faith of their forebears. Most of them were once "good Soviet kids" who, like many of us, found emptiness in the world.

"The Party gave me an appreciation for justice, but it failed me in Spirit," said Volodya, once a member of *Komsomol,* a youth cadre run according to Party principles. Volodya at one time aspired to the Party in imitation of his father and older brother, both Communists. He eventually, at twenty-four, turned to the church instead. "I accept, still, many of the political principles — to be a capitalist and a Christian involves contradiction I couldn't bear," he protests. "But I came to the church to find food for the soul. My father and my brother, of course, can't understand. They think I'm in another century. But my grandmother and uncle," he smiles, "think it's great."

Volodya's close colleagues at work know he is a believer and respect his convictions. "In socialism we achieve many goals," he professes, "but without God we cannot hope to penetrate the center of justice."

To go to confession in the Soviet Union brings into sharp focus the nature and trials of being a Christian. In a midsized provincial town during a month-long trip one recent summer, I went to confession to a very busy priest who had just finished a long line of baptisms. You must understand that confession for an Orthodox Christian is of two kinds: frequently we receive absolution, simply a cleansing acknowledgment of forgiveness, before we receive the Eucharist. Much less often, we engage in a prolonged, private face-to-face confession. I had chosen to go to private confession.

The first question the priest asked me, not recognizing me as an American, was: "Did you ever deny God or deny your faithfulness to him?" The question was in an offhand drone. Clearly, it was a question of great frequency. When I said I had not, the priest raised an eyebrow and scrutinized me more closely: "Are you from another republic?" (He expected me to be from one of the Baltic republics, perhaps, where the situation of believers is somewhat less constrained.) When we settled into the details of my spiritual life, he gave me kind, patient, and good counsel. In the midst of our talk, however, he sniffed the smell of tobacco. "Do you smoke?" he asked. I nodded—to my knowledge, our faith did not prohibit smoking. "No more," he said. "Not here in Russia. You are a believer." Going without nicotine was my pathetic reflection of the hard choices Russian Christians make.

The situation of believers in Russia is a complex, many-faceted tale. By no means is the Orthodox Church in Russia a hotbed of dissent. Nor is it a cowering reflection of Kremlin policy. It is an expression of God's kingdom, not ours. And intemperate, righteous indignation at the situation of believers in Russia can hold the church hostage.

Of course the state resists the faith. The state openly espouses an atheistic doctrine. We cannot forget that, any more than we can forget that our own state espouses materialist, self-aggrandizing principles no less hostile to faith. Yet to use believers in Russia as ammunition in a propaganda battle endangers our brothers and sisters there as much as anything else.

We should encourage our American press to silence its stridency. We should quell our righteous indignation and listen quietly for a moment to what these believers can teach us. First of all, they can teach us the soul of ecumenism. Orthodox believers, without sacrificing who they are, express love for other Christians.

Vilnius in Lithuania has a strong Catholic presence and a working Orthodox monastery. There is a profound sense of community among Christians in that vigorously believing city. One gracious woman, a devout Catholic with a deep devotion to the Orthodox St. Seraphim and a smiling portrait of John Paul II pinned up in her kitchen, is the focus for a small community of sharing believers. When I asked her why a mutual friend in Moscow had thought she was an Orthodox Christian, she chided me, "My dear, in Vilnius I was born. Here I am a Catholic. But Moscow is an Orthodox city. Wherever we live, we are God's workers." When I reminded her that bishops, Catholic or Orthodox, might object to her idea of faith by geography, she waved the reminder away with a spoon. "I love our bishops," she smiled, "but I also know human nature. It is divine nature we must obey."

Russian believers can teach us something about a Christian stance toward disarmament. No Russian Christian I know sees nuclear arms as anything but the work of Satan. There is no self-excusing justification among them for a balance of terror. It is revealing to worship with those who feel threatened by us in the United States. When American missiles point at a friend and his children, it is difficult to argue, "Hey, that's O.K. Remember, we're the good guys."

Despite the antireligious bias of their government, Russian Christians see our government as a danger. They are acutely aware that we are the party who actually used the bomb, who will not promise not to do it again, and who will see them, after all, as its primary targets. The Soviet press publicizes, accurately, the statements of Christian nuclear apologists. When Jerry Falwell speaks, he creates for Soviet Christians the model of a Christian pastor who would hold over their children the threat of incineration.

American Christians, then, can reach out to their counterparts in the Soviet Union. In no way do I wish to detract from the sufferings and imprisonment imposed on Russian believers who fall afoul of the authorities. Nor, in my discussion of Orthodox believers, do I wish to detract from the greater problems of evangelicals. Those who wish to actually help, comfort, and even contact Russian Christian prisoners and their families may do so through an excellent organization, the Society of St. Stephen, Box

52, Athens, Illinois, 62613.

I do wish to argue, however, that it is a greater good to reach out in an effort to understand than it is to use the sufferings of Russian Christians, few of whom would accept our *political* presumptions, as justifications for our own political positions. We Christians, sensitive to evil, are sometimes too ready to place it elsewhere. It is the intense hostility between our two countries, and the hatred that we so often glibly fuel, that embodies an evil greater than that contained in either one of us.

In explaining the differences between Eastern and Western Christians, I remember what an earnest young Orthodox physicist said in a small discussion among Catholics and Orthodox, late at night, in one of the vast apartment complexes on the edge of Moscow. "You in the West, it seems to me, aim somehow for the breadth of the gospel. In worship, in social movements, you seem to want to stretch outward. We Orthodox here in Russia are more vertically oriented. We strive for depth, we 'dive' for the Spirit. We try to find that center from which radiates the divine energy."

The two movements, vertical and horizontal, create of Christendom a vast and saving cross. May we be as faithful to our role in its work as the believers in Russia are to theirs.

Meeting the Soviet People

Richard Baggett Deats

Five of us from the Volga Peace Cruise were walking along the streets of Ulyanovsk, looking in all the store windows. We were obviously American, with cameras around our necks and peace buttons in English and Russian. A man in a suit and tie and carrying a suitcase became excited when he saw us. He stopped to talk, in halting English. He had been in the Red Army during the Great Patriotic War (or World War II, as we call it), remembered fondly the American allies then, and was worried now that our two countries seemed headed for war. He wished to welcome us to his country and to tell us to assure our people back home that the Soviet people want peace. He took us to the kiosk and bought us each an ice cream cone. Then he took us to the Lenin Museum, the pride of this city, Lenin's birthplace. There he bought us each a set of color postcards and a badge bearing the name of Ulyanovsk. Then he left, heading back to his work as an engineer.

This chance meeting is typical of almost every place I've visited in the Soviet Union. Time and again the friendliness and generosity of people whom I had expected, before going to Russia, to be somewhat dour and reserved, struck me. Some fit my expectations, of course, but my strongest impressions are of those who responded positively to our presence as ambassadors of peace. Peace and friendship — *mir e druzhba* — especially evoke warmth from this people who have known so much war and deprivation in their history. The nine-hundred-day siege of Leningrad, the scorched earth of the Ukraine and Byelorussia, the carnage of Stalingrad — such terrors are living memories to the Soviets from World War II. Scarcely a town can be found without some monument to that war and people eager to talk at length on the need for peace.

In Volgograd (Stalingrad until it was renamed in Khrushchev's de-Stalinization campaign) we visited Mamayev Hill on which a decisive battle was fought that cost the lives of nearly one million Germans and Soviets. Our guide was Ruisa, who was only three when the war came. Alone with her mother (her father was in the army), they decided to flee Stalingrad when the German divisions neared the city. They crossed the Volga River and hid until the fighting was over. When they returned, their home was gone, the city destroyed. Ruisa and her mother dug a shelter in the ground where they lived for many months. They helped rebuild their city, now a modern, bustling center of education and industry, but they cannot forget what they have been through. Following the Soviet custom, we placed flowers on the memorial as a gesture of hope that the scourge of war would not come again. "When you see what we have been through," said Ruisa, "can you ever doubt that having peace is the most precious and important thing in all the world to us?"

Doubt it I cannot — though I grieve that the average Soviet citizen (like, alas, the average American) champions an uncritical patriotism. They believe "peace through strength" is the only way to have that warless future. Yet if only Americans could begin to see the sincerity and passion with which the Soviets speak of peace, and understand what they've been through, perhaps we would be more willing to take steps to build trust between our two peoples.

I think of another unexpected meeting, this one in Kiev, the park-filled capital of the Ukraine. One of our group was in a department store trying to buy some hand-painted wooden eggs. Surrounded by a crowd of shoppers, she asked if anyone could speak English. A young man answered and helped her make her purchase.

Later that evening a group of us met the young man, Sasha, and two of his friends in the park. They took us on a walking tour of the city till past midnight. All evening we asked questions of each other, each revealing our misperceptions of the other's land. The young men were students in the Naval Academy and Communist Party members. Sasha particularly loved American literature and history. He was perplexed that more Americans did not study his land and his people's literature and language. We later found that there are more Russians *teaching* English than Americans *studying* Russian! Others of our group were startled to learn that the United States was one of fourteen Western nations to invade the Soviet Union after the Revolution in order "to strangle Bolshevism in the cradle," as Winston Churchill so graphically put it.

We ended the evening at the outskirts of the city, in the apartment of Sasha's family. Although we arrived unannounced at midnight, we were warmly greeted and served apples and Hungarian wine. Sasha played a Bach cantata for us on the record player and showed us family photos. Finally, we went out looking for a taxi to go back to the hotel. We walked across the bridge spanning the Dnieper River, absorbed in a searching and animated theological discussion. Sasha insisted on paying the taxi fare as we parted with embraces, pledging our friendship despite differences in belief about God, the meaning of freedom, and a host of other things.

Another person I'll always remember is Valery, our Intourist guide in Minsk, the capital of Byelorussia. Unlike some of our guides, he is a Communist Party member and highly interested in political issues. A Byelorussian patriot, he helped us understand the separate history and identity of the Byelorussian people, who have their own language, culture, and traditions distinct from that of the Russians. A nation eleven hundred years old, it has been destroyed eight times in its history. Valery loves Byelorussia's greatest poet, Yangka Kapala, who wrote poetry in his native language even though it was forbidden under the czars. In front of Kapala's statue in a lovely park, Valery recited by heart long stanzas of the poet's works.

When we went to the war memorial at nearby Khatyn, Valery gave us a powerful sense of the suffering of the Byelorussians. They lost a quarter of their people during the last war. There, too, he recited poetry to us:

People of good will, remember:
We loved life, our motherland, and you, the people
We were devoured by the fire of death
We appeal to all of you
May your sorrow and grief turn into courage and strength
So that everlasting peace can be established on earth forever
    after

So that never again will life be devoured by the vortex of fire and
death.

We couldn't help but feel a close rapport with Valery as we exchanged ideas about politics, nuclear war, and the future of our
two peoples.

I remember, too, my surprise when talking with our guide in
Leningrad. She said that, though she is an atheist, whenever she has
serious problems she goes into a church, lights a candle, and
reflects in the silence.

A young boy began walking beside me in Kazan as I strolled
along the Volga looking at the ships. Every time I looked at him, he
would look shyly away till, with a burst of courage, he came over
and handed me a post card of his hometown and seemed overwhelmed when I gave him a peace button, shook his hand, and
said, *"Mir e druzba."*

And there was the journalist from Pravda who had been in the
Red Army division that met the American Army on the Elbe River
in Germany in World War II. "I don't like capitalism and you don't
like Communism," he said, "but we live on an endangered planet
that mustn't have another war. Next time there will be nothing left
—no birds to sing, no flowers for the dead. Our peoples must have
peace together."

Whatever our differences—and they are real—that journalist
was right. Nothing can justify another war. Everything is at stake,
even the future of the planet. And when you think about it, we've
been far too conscious of how we are different and how our
systems clash. The time has come to strengthen our common links
as God's children.

My Love Affair With the Soviet People

Carol Pendell

What are the Soviet people really like? Very much like
Americans! They come in all shapes and sizes. They come from a
variety of ethnic backgrounds that gives a lovely diversity to facial
features. They come from cities, towns, and rural villages; from
climates that are warm and welcoming or frigid and forbidding.

They live in a country so vast that it encompasses one-sixth of
the earth's land surface, it contains fertile agricultural areas, semi-
arid plains (steppes), coastal areas, great rivers, majestic mountains, tundra—a land as diverse as its people.

They are a remarkable people, warm and wonderful, strong and resilient, with a great capacity for love and joy. I have been having a love affair with the Soviet people since 1958!

Let me share with you the story of a young couple we met at that time. He was an engineer, she an engineering student. We had spent many hours together walking the streets of their beautiful city and talking about the meaning of life, the future of our two countries, what life was like for each of us. Then we were invited to their home for tea. Their city had known great devastation in the Second World War, so housing was still difficult to find. They shared a tiny room with her mother. Three families used the kitchen and bath. But they felt more fortunate than many others. They at least had a bathtub — though they could not afford to buy wood to heat the water. But in that home we found love and concern, not only for one another but the world. While we were there, her mother returned from work. Gathering me in her arms and pressing her face to mine, she said, "Americanski, Americanski!" We were both in tears.

Writing to us a month later, my two friends said, "It is good the tourist exchange is taking place. The peoples of our countries are getting opportunities to learn more and more about each other. That will be very important for establishing more friendly relations between our countries and understanding between the peoples, and it means peace. We keep with care in our hearts every recollection about you, dear folks! We guess, maybe after some time, you will be able to come to the U.S.S.R. Then we'll be happy to see you again, our beloved friends! We frequently think and speak of you. Some evenings we think 'Perhaps Carol is now sending the boys to school.' When it is evening here, you already have morning. Imagine, how far we are from each other, but how close are our hearts!" How close are our hearts!

Editors note:

In receiving this contribution I have become aware that Carol Pendell, president of the Women's International League for Peace and Freedom, embodies a remarkable story of friendship. After fourteen trips to the Soviet Union she is reluctant to write her most precious experiences because she could betray the trust of those who allowed her to be a part of their private lives. She believes, however, that her experiences have shattered the myth of the less-than-human Russian. Rooted deeply in the life of the church, she has long been convinced that the personal gospel and the social gospel are but two sides of the same coin. Yet this unique opportunity to pursue her love affair with the Soviet people has come after raising three sons as the wife of a Methodist minister.

In 1979 Carol Pendell founded the U.S.A.-U.S.S.R. Citizens' Dialogue. The seed for these exchanges came out of a conversation with Madame Zinaida Kruglova, head of the All-Union Society for Friendship and Cultural Relations in Russia. While strolling through Disneyland in 1977, this Russian woman said at one point, "Our governments don't seem to be making the kind of progress they ought to make. Perhaps the peoples in our two countries could get together and talk about ways to end the arms race."

Pendell explains that the Citizens' Dialogue, in which thirty citizens of one country host citizens of the other in homes and at a conference, is based on a "nonconfrontational stance in which we believe in the right of each country to pursue the kind of economic, political, social, and cultural life that is their own. It is our responsibility to find areas in which we can work together. We have to build a climate in which meaningful arms reduction talks can take place."

Don Clark, a retired U.S. Air Force colonel, participated in one of the first exchanges. He denies any hint of brainwashing. But he does report how radically some of his perceptions changed through dialogue with the Soviet people. "I went to Russia with profound misgivings and a certainty that their system directly threatened our very survival. I left with a vastly changed outlook. I saw that the threat idea is so exaggerated my fear evaporated on the spot."

Currently, the idea of these exchanges is catching on. Many other groups are making similar plans. Hearing of this greatly increased activity, Carol said, "Let a thousand flowers bloom."

Moscow International Book Fair

Clyde Weaver

Many American book publishers refused to travel to the biennial International Book Fair in the Soviet Union in 1983. In this way they protested Soviet treatment of its dissident authors.

The Protestant Church-Owned Publishing Association I represented believed our books had something to offer that might mitigate against the harsh realities of our divided world. Though many publishers boycotted the fair, one of the participating publishers said, "It does us little good to sit on our haunches and make ugly faces across the waters."

We often forget the hundred million Christians and over three million Jews who live in the Soviet Union, though we have many historical religious bonds to them. Avoiding contacts with these people will not help in their, or our, search for peace. The degree to which we turn these hardy Russians into something less than equals as human beings is eye-opening. After a forceful declamation to some recently-ousted Soviet writers outlining why a well known New York publisher spurned the book fair, one speaker reinforced his premise by stating that he was afraid an American presence might endanger dissident Russian writers. To this an exiled Soviet author replied, "This is a risk for us to decide."

Another Soviet writer chided, "Words are a magic weapon for peace. By going and showing your books, you get some of them into the hands of the people. That makes an opening in the armor of the state. And don't make the mistake of identifying the state with the people."

I knew almost nothing about Russian publishing when I made the trip. After observing people reading worn and tattered volumes, I ventured to ask one woman how old her book was, thinking it surely must be an antique. But when I saw the recent publishing date, I realized the book had passed through dozens and dozens of hands in a very few years. The Soviets don't just read books; they consume them. Ninety-five percent of all books printed are sold within the first year of publication. Studies have shown that seventy percent of the Soviet people prefer reading to all other spare-time activities. Ninety per cent of all families have a home library. Men, women, and children can be found avidly reading in subways and buses, and on park benches. Four thousand libraries in Moscow, fifteen thousand bookstores and thirty-five thousand kiosks (sidewalk booths) in the entire country try to feed this fascination with the printed page. The book fair draws around a hundred thousand visitors over a period of seven days. We were so overwhelmed by the multitude of people that there was little time to see the book booths of the ninety-two other countries represented. The Soviet press indicated that our spot was one of the most visited in the entire fair.

Our major attraction was a replica of a huge Bible first printed in Russia in 1908. Visitors would touch it, photograph it, kiss it, and caress it. As they crowded around this symbol of their past, our spot soon became known to our Russian friends as the "Bible booth."

The stories of our experiences in our crowded booth would fill a book. One day an elderly woman came up to me, gently picked up the Bible, turned to the two pages of the Book of Obadiah, and announced to the group surrounding her that they should read it immediately. After they had read intently for five minutes, she said. "Now go and remember you have read God's word!" In the United States such an order might have fallen on deaf ears; not so in Russia that day.

I knew Russians love buttons and insignia, so I had brought with me twelve hundred embroidered stickers depicting the world in blue with a white dove superimposed on it. I passed them out as gifts. Those who received them accepted them eagerly. One woman to whom I had given a sticker on a crowded subway train got up from her seat and insisted that I sit in her seat.

An earnest young radio operator came up and told us in English about his desire for more communication between our countries. He wanted me to be sure to tell the American people that Russians wanted more exchanges with them. After I had talked with him for forty-five minutes, he concluded by saying, "I sincerely appreciate your being here." Then he added, "My favorite American song goes something like this: 'Everyone has a hungry heart. Nobody wants to be left apart.'"

One of the men who visited our booth told me he had written his Ph.D. dissertation on the economic system of the United States. He and his wife, a writer for a well-known Soviet magazine, invited me to their apartment. With their school age daughter, I enjoyed a fine Russian meal and many hours of stimulating discussion.

One of my more unusual experiences was being interviewed by Soviet national TV. The announcers knew I had brought with me a scroll two thousand members of the Church of the Brethren had signed at their annual conference. With it was a letter, addressed to President Andropov, urging the Soviets to become partners with us in a search for world peace.

After reading from the letter, the interviewers asked me two interesting questions: "What is the significance of books in a technological age?" and "How do you feel about world peace?"

I answered, "Books give people time to reflect and review. They give readers the chance to reread, underline, assimilate, and argue with the ideas presented. Thoughts freely expressed can stimulate more insights, not for destruction — but for dialogue. We need books to get and stay in touch with one another."

To the second question, a mind-boggling one, I answered, "We need to see our differences as having integrity. Because we have a pluralistic society in the United States, we should be able to move about easily in a world that requires pluralistic living. Differences can enrich and energize. They can build or destroy."

One afternoon I visited an official of the Russian Orthodox Church. We sat down in his reception room for a visit. One observation he made gave me pause. He suggested that as a people with an extensive history, the Russians are war-worn and experienced with the ways of many rulers. In America, on the other hand, we were in the teen years of our governmental history and organization.

"Perhaps," he said, "there is something you can learn from us as well as something we can learn from you."

I breathed a prayer that we as historical teen-agers in this world could share our great ideals with greater love and humility. As I reflect on my visits to the Soviet Union, I know more about the universal nature of God's church in the world. "For God so loved the *world*. . . " has no nationalistic boundaries and supports no one economic system. God's love is equally available to everyone. The church in Russia is alive sixty-seven years after a political revolution whose official goal was to eliminate all religious concepts. You see spiritual life in the people's faces. You can hear it as they sing and preach. You can experience it as they invite you into their homes and hearts. You can feel it in their deep longing for peace.

After a church service in the Moscow Baptist Church, a small group from our publishing booth met together with the officers and administrators of the church for a meal. As we shared stories of our faith and ate their delicious food, we felt part of God's world family. Before we left, we held hands and sang, "Blest be the tie that binds our hearts in Christian love. . . ." That tie surmounts all political and economic differences.

Homecoming
Katherine L. Weaver

Deep in the black earth region of the Ukraine my husband and I stood and conversed with an Intourist official. Slowly we were facing the realization that Soviet regulations required a thirty days notice for deviations from a given itinerary. (Soviet citizens who visit the United States have similiar restrictions.) Our travels had brought us to the spot from which we wished to take a short trip to the ancestral home of my great-grandfather on the Sea of Azov. Months earlier we had thought of including this in our plans. We decided, however, that it was probably not necessary to request a sixty-mile extension. Noting our distress, the official offered to take us to a closer site where the first Mennonite settlement in Russia had been. Later, and quite by accident, we discovered he had cancelled an important engagement to give us this personal tour.

Part of the early Chortitza colony had been situated on an island in the Dnieper River. Catherine the Great had offered this land to the beleaguered Anabaptists of Western Europe in 1786 in the hope they would stabilize the "wild fields" so often overrun by marauding outsiders and depleted by inconstant tenants.

In this place the Mennonites had built a teacher's college, presently being used as a high school. As the three of us approached the building, a tall, beautifully dressed, blond woman came out the front door and asked, in excellent English, if she could help us. Hearing how far we had traveled, she urged us to come in. After seeing several classrooms, we sat together with her, the instructor of earth sciences, and the school's principal discussing the reason for our trip. I was intrigued with their excitement, and one statement in particular struck me.

As I told them of the efforts we had made to reach the seaport of Berdyansk where my great-grandfather, Cornelius Jansen, a grain merchant, had lived, one of the women looked at me and exclaimed, "Why it's just as if you're coming home!" Jansen had been banished by the Czar in 1873, so Russia had never seemed to be an even remote homeland to me, but in that moment of exclamation, a sense of homecoming touched me deeply.

As we remember now, our entire three-thousand-kilometer trip was filled with various individuals' attempts to make us feel at home. We marvel that we were allowed to rent a car and travel the equivalent of eighteen hundred miles without a guide, although we couldn't speak Russian, much less read the country's road signs.

Ironically, when the opportunity to visit Moscow for the International Fair was offered, I did not want to go. My husband, as marketing director for a publishing house, was both personally and professionally enthusiastic. My thinking was: plane travel is claustrophobic; visas may not come on time; how can one crush all needed clothing and other items for a twenty-day stay into one underseat bag? I must ask for time off from work; etc. Then irritating trivialities sank into perspective, and I decided the trip was an opportunity not to be missed.

We asked for an itinerary that would take us to southern Russia first. The balance of our time would then be spent in Moscow at the Book Fair. We were unaware that two United States citizens taking a trip of such length alone was not often allowed.

So, oblivious to obstacles, we plunged ahead.

In our rented car we spent nine hours the first day on the road and traveled only a hundred and twenty-two miles. We had awakened early for this long-anticipated trip and asked for our passports. After lengthly and uncertain replies as to their whereabouts, the woman at the hotel desk finally told us we would have to wait for the proper person. At last, with official papers in hand, we arrived at the car rental office. There a Mr. Romanov told us our travel was not authorized to begin until the next day. After clearing up that potential delay, we probed our way out of Moscow. Beyond the city we found ourselves on roads so crowded with a variety of vehicles traveling at widely different rates of speed that we were reminded of Chicago expressways at rush hour. Once, all traffic came to an abrupt halt. We crept along for miles until we reached the source of the obstruction. A funeral procession was moving along on foot as young people scattered evergreen boughs on the road from a leading truck. It was a fitting and solemn ceremony, and we felt chastened for our irritation.

Later, nearing our night's destination, we became thoroughly disoriented and stopped to ask directions. Through a confusion of German, Russian, and English we had an introduction to the hospitality of the people we were to encounter on this trip. Searching the past for my long unused German, I listened with great care as a German-speaking Russian invited us to follow his friend in a truck. We did so for some distance. Taking us on less traveled roads, he stopped in a small village, parked his truck, and returned to our car. From his vantage point in the back seat he guided us to our hotel with urgent hand signals.

As we sat in the lobby exhausted from our journey, the Intourist representative came to us and expressed her pleasure at our visit. Again and again we received such thoughtful responses, particularly when lost, which was often. People would cluster about us and try to help continue our trip. Sometimes maps were drawn in the dust, others were sketched with pencil on scraps of paper. Not infrequently someone would point to our car, get in, and gesture us along our way. One time when our battery refused to function, a bus driver brought distilled water and worked until it was operational. On another occasion our parked car needed to be moved to make way for heavy machinery. Several men, unable to contact us, lifted and slid it out of the way. The distant place from which we had come in our wish to visit was to these people a constant source of amazement and delight. We encountered it over and over. It was our greeting.

An air of sadness constricted this sense of homecoming, however. To my dismay, stealthy reminders of past wars intruded at unexpected intervals. Vast constructions — over six thousand apartments a day — were piecing together a still partially shattered country.

We were surprised at the lack of suspicion and wariness toward us. Before leaving the United States much had been said about reactivating the neutron bomb. Because this weapon kills everything that lives and leaves all which is inanimate intact, the young woman who offered to show us Turgenev's former estate wistfully wondered aloud if buildings and mineral wealth were of more value than human life.

Students expressed their uneasiness with the instability in the world. Older people spoke of starvation and desperation in their youth. Eternal flames, guarded by honor students, gave chilling testimony to twenty million war dead.

On one occasion, perhaps frivolously, and certainly in ignorance, I asked an English-speaking European if Russian gourmet cook books were generally available and used. He replied, "Most people are simply pleased that there is enough good food to eat. Elegant dining is not a priority item for most. Maybe someday."

As for the two of us, we received something more lasting than elegant dining. Out of what these people had they eagerly gave. We ask ourselves today, "Would we have done as much?" We also ask, "Can this world become a home for all, in which we simply live in different rooms and meet as friends? Or will we divide this home so it becomes an unfit place for anyone to live?"

Part II

WHY DO WE FEAR THE RUSSIANS?

In arms race discussions, the question inevitably emerges: what about those Russians? It is assumed they are out to bury us, to export their style of revolutionary terrorism around the world. The worst possible scenario would be to live under Soviet rule. These fears have shaped our national priorities, foreign policy, and responses. The mirror image is reflected by the Russian government. They fear us as much as or more than we fear them.

Are these fears justified? Are both sides brainwashed with propaganda by powerful interest groups? Mutual exchanges reveal that Americans and Russians share friendly and generous characteristics and a great capacity for joy and love. Both peoples are conditioned to think well of the other at the same time the government of the opposing superpower is judged to be bad. Are we destined to continue to live by these assumptions?

There are no easy answers. One contribution of this book might be to question the most simple answers in order to facilitate changes in attitudes. Chapters 4, 5, and 6 deal respectively with Soviet intentions and capabilities and the Soviet threat to freedom.

Two veteran peacemakers interpret the intentions of Soviet leaders. Few Americans can match George Kennan's experience in dealing with Russian leaders. His service extended over a twenty-year period in the American embassy in Moscow before he became our ambassador to Russia and subsequently to Yugoslavia. With permission we offer a major portion of one of Kennan's articles entitled "Reflections: Two Views of the Soviet Problem" (New Yorker, November 2, 1981). Here he contrasts his own analyses of Soviet intentions with prevailing views in official circles.

John Swomley, a veteran civil rights and peace activist, examines basic myths about Soviet intentions. He writes out of a background of years of striving to apply Christian ethics to global concerns. Swomley offers a challenging counterpoint to many popular sentiments.

In the second part of the above article Kennan responds to those who view the Soviets to be ahead in the arms race.

> I am only a private citizen. I do not have access to all the information at the disposition of the governments. But, with all respect for the sincerity and good faith of those who advance this view, I am disinclined to accept it just on the basis of their say-so. I am so disinclined because I think I have made a reasonable effort in this last

few years to follow such information as appears in the press and other media about the military balance, and I find this body of information confused, contradictory, statistically questionable, and often misleading.

Out of deep concern Sister Pam Solo has given over a decade to specialize in this kind of information. As a staff member of the American Friends Service Committee she is regarded as an authority on the statistics and nature of the arms race. She combines a historical perspective with moral guidance. Many have failed to comprehend the major shift in weapons systems the last few years. Though our military headquarters is still named the Department of Defense, our weapons are increasingly designed for offense. Sister Solo documents this shift from a strategy of deterrence, which has been dubbed MAD (mutually assured destruction), to counterforce or first-strike strategy, which can be designated INSANE (immediate nuclear strike anticipating nuclear exchange).

My experiences in the Soviet Union forced me to struggle with my views of freedom. The issue first emerged when I spent a day with a Moscow taxi driver. From our conversations it was obvious that he had little political interest. His primary preoccupations were rock music, women, and racing. It occurred to me that he was as free to pursue his interests as is his counterpart in the United States. In fact, he may be a bit more free, for I could not imagine his being able to practice racing on the job as enthusiastically on the crowded streets of any major American city. In another conversation a Russian claimed that a Baptist in Moscow was freer to go to church on Sunday night than a Baptist in New York City. He seemed very aware of the fear of mugging that frightens many Americans.

After relating personal encounters with violations of human rights, Ken Brown discusses the contrasting views of freedom between our two systems. It was in listening to some Russian views that I was forced to stretch mine. Soviets fear the autonomy of the individual, which can destroy the well-being of society. If one person is allowed to control half the oil of Texas, it is argued, the freedom of many to have their share is taken away. Americans fear any society that represses civil liberties. The Soviets focus on economic rights, the right of each person to have adequate medical care, enough to eat, and a place to live. Americans feature the political rights of free speech and assembly. Both sides are quick to name the sins of the other. The Soviets are very aware of our ghettos; we are outraged by their work or concentration camps. Ken Brown calls on us to transcend the posture of self-righteousness long enough to learn from one another.

4

ARE THEY OUT TO BURY US?

Two Views of the Soviet Problem

George Kennan

Looking back over the whole course of the differences between my own view of East-West relations and the views of my various critics and opponents in recent years, I have to conclude that the differences have been, essentially, not ones of interpretation of phenomena whose reality we all agree on but, rather, differences over the nature and significance of the observable phenomena themselves—in other words, differences not about the meaning of what we see but, rather, about what it is that we see in the first place.

Let me illustrate this first with the example of our differing views of the nature of the Soviet regime.

My opponents, if I do not misinterpret their position, see the Soviet leaders as a group of men animated primarily by a desire to achieve further expansion of their effective power, and this at the expense of the independence and the liberties of other people—at the expense of the stability, and perhaps the peace, of international life. They see these men as pursuing a reckless and gigantic build-up of their own armed forces—a build-up of such dimensions that it cannot be explained by defensive considerations alone and must therefore, it is reasoned, reflect aggressive ones. They see them as eager to bring other countries, in the Third World and elsewhere, under their domination, in order to use those countries as pawns against the United States and other nations of the Western alliance; and they see the situations existing today in such places as Angola and Ethiopia and Afghanistan as examples of the dangerous success of these endeavors. My opponents reject the suggestion that Soviet policy might be motivated in any important degree by defensive considerations. In their view, the Soviet leaders do not feel politically encircled or in any other ways significantly threatened. And though it is recognized that Moscow faces serious internal problems, it is not thought that these problems impose any very serious limitation on the freedom of the regime to pursue aggressive external intentions. What emerges from this vision is, of course, an image of the Soviet regime not greatly different from the image of the Nazi regime as it existed shortly before the outbreak of the Second World War. This being the case, it is not surprising that the conclusion should be drawn that the main task for Western statesmanship at this time must be to avoid what are now generally regarded as the great mistakes of the Western powers in the late 1930s; that is, to avoid what is called appeasement, to give a low priority to the possibilities for negotiation and accommodation, and to concentrate on the building up of a military posture so imposing and forbidding, and a Western unity so unshakable, that the Soviet leaders will perceive the futility and the danger of their aggressive plans, and will accept the necessity of learning to live side by side with other nations on a basis compatible with the security of those other nations and with the general requirements of world stability and peace. I do not question the good faith of American governmental personalities when they say that, once this new relationship of military and political power has been established, they will be prepared to sit down with their Soviet counterparts and discuss with them the prerequisites for a safer world; but I fear they see the success of any such discussions as something to which the Soviet leaders could be brought only reluctantly, with gnashing of teeth, and this seems to me to be a poor augury for the lasting quality of any results that might be achieved.

Now, all this, as I say, is what I believe my opponents see when they turn their eyes in the direction of the Kremlin. What I see is something quite different. I see a group of troubled men — elderly men, for the most part — whose choices and possibilities are severely constrained. I see these men as prisoners of many circumstances: prisoners of their own past and their country's past; prisoners of the antiquated ideology to which their extreme sense of orthodoxy binds them; prisoners of the rigid system of power that has given them their authority; but prisoners, too, of certain ingrained peculiarities of the Russian statemanship of earlier ages — the congenital sense of insecurity, the lack of inner self-confidence, the distrust of the foreigner and the foreigner's world, the passion for secrecy, the neurotic fear of penetration by other powers into areas close to their borders, and a persistent tendency, resulting from all these other factors, to overdo the creation of military strength. I see here men deeply preoccupied, as were their Czarist Russian predecessors, with questions of prestige—preoccupied more, in many instances, with the appearances than with the realities. I do not see them as men anxious to expand their power by the direct use of their armed forces, although they could easily be frightened into taking actions that would seem to have this aim. I see them as indeed concerned—and rather naturally concerned—to increase their influence among Third World countries. This neither surprises me nor alarms me. Most great powers have similar desires. And the methods adopted by the Soviet Union are not very different from those adopted by some of the others. Besides, what has distinguished these Soviet efforts, historically viewed, seems to be not their success but precisely their lack of it. I see no recent Soviet achievements in this direction that would remotely outweigh the great failures of the postwar period: in Yugoslavia, in China, and in Egypt.

But, beyond that, a wish to expand one's *influence* is not the same thing as a wish to expand the formal limits of one's power and responsibility. This I do not think the Soviet leaders at all wish to do. Specifically, I have seen no evidence that they are at all disposed to invade Western Europe and thereby to take any further parts of it formally under their authority. They are having trouble enough with the responsibilities they have already undertaken in Eastern Europe. They have no reason to wish to increase these burdens. I can conceive that there might be certain European regions, outside the limits of their present hegemony, where they would be happy, for defensive purposes, to have some sort of military control, if such control could be acquired safely and easily, without severe disruption of international stability; but it is a far cry from this to the assumption that they would be disposed to invade any of these areas out of the blue, in peacetime, at the cost of unleashing another world war.

It is my belief that these men do indeed consider the Soviet Union to have been increasingly isolated and in danger of encirclement by hostile powers in recent years. I do not see how they could otherwise interpret the American military relationship with Iran in the time of the Shah or the more recent American military relationships with Pakistan and China. And these, I believe, are not the only considerations that would limit the freedom of the Soviet leaders to indulge themselves in dreams of external expansion, even if they were inclined toward such dreams. They are obviously very conscious of the dangers of a disintegration of their dominant position in Eastern Europe, and particularly in Poland; and this not because they have any conscious desire to mistreat or oppress the peoples involved but because they see any further deterioration of the situation there as a threat to their political and strategic interests in Germany—interests that are unquestionably highly defensive in origin.

I believe, too, that internal developments in the Soviet Union present a heavy claim on the attention and the priorities of the Soviet leaders. They are deeply committed to the completion of their existing programs for the economic and social development of the Soviet peoples, and I am sure that they are very seriously concerned over the numerous problems that have recently been impeding that completion: the perennial agricultural failures; the many signs of public apathy, demoralization, drunkenness, and labor absenteeism; the imbalance in population growth between the Russian center and the non-Russian periphery; the increasing shortage of skilled labor; and the widespread economic corruption and indiscipline. They may differ among themselves as to how these problems should be approached, but I doubt whether there are any of them who think that the problems could be solved by the unleashing of another world war. I emphatically reject the primitive thesis, drawn largely from misleading and outdated nineteenth-century examples, that the Kremlin might be inclined to resort to war as a means of resolving its internal difficulties. Nothing in Russian history or psychology supports such a thesis.

In saying these things, I do not mean to deny that there exist, interwoven with the rest of the pattern of Soviet diplomacy, certain disquieting tendencies, which oblige Western policymakers to exercise a sharp vigilance even as they pursue their efforts toward peace. I believe that these tendencies reflect not so much any thirst for direct aggression as an oversuspiciousness, a fear of being tricked or outsmarted, an exaggerated sense of prestige, and an interpretation of Russia's defensive needs so extreme—so extravagant and so far-reaching—that it becomes in itself a threat, or an apparent threat, to the security of other nations. While these weaknesses probably affect all Soviet statesmen to one extent or another, the evidence suggests to me that they are concentrated particularly in specific elements of the Soviet power structure—notably, in the military and naval commands, in the vast police establishment, and in certain sections of the Party apparatus. So far, these tendencies do not seem to me to have dominated Soviet policy, except in the case of the decision to intervene in Afghanistan—a decision that was taken in somewhat abnormal circumstances and is now, I believe, largely recognized, even in Moscow, as a mistake. But there will soon have to be extensive changes in the occupancy of the senior political positions in Moscow, and Western policymakers should consider that a Western policy that offers no encouragement to the more moderate elements in the Soviet hierarchy must inevitably strengthen the hand, and the political position, of those who are not moderate at all.

The Myths of Soviet Intentions

John M. Swomley, Jr.

Millions of Americans are now convinced that the arms race has to be stopped. We need to reduce, and eventually to eliminate, the nuclear weapons that threaten the survival of human and other life on our planet.

The major obstacle blocking a rapid and reasonable solution to the arms race is fear of the Soviet Union. Americans have been conditioned by both events and propaganda to believe the Soviets intend to conquer the world. They think Russians cannot be trusted to negotiate arms reduction or keep treaties that have been negotiated. They feel Russian arms build-up is not a response to their own fears but a way to achieve world hegemony.

The events that have created American fear include the Soviet occupation of Eastern Europe during World War II and the later armed intervention in Hungary, Czechoslovakia, and Afghanistan. The purpose of this intervention was to maintain control over states that wanted greater independence. Other events that frighten Americans include totalitarian Soviet control over its citizens, the denial of human rights to dissenters, and the provision of weapons and military technicians to such countries as Cuba and Syria.

The propaganda that causes our fear of the Soviet Union began in 1917 when the Bolshevik revolution succeeded in Russia. American business and political leaders immediately understood that the revolution provided a moral and practical alternative to the imperialism of the day. That imperialism included both the British-French form of political colonialism and the American variety, corporations that were expanding their investments in and control over other countries. The victorious nations following World War I decided to contain Communism by a belt of countries, a *cordon sanitaire,* that in Clemenceau's words was established "to isolate the West from the germs of Bolshevism in the East."

President Franklin D. Roosevelt reversed the policy of

isolating the Soviet Union. He recognized that nation prior to World War II and made a wartime alliance with the British and the Soviets against Nazi Germany. After Roosevelt's death Harry Truman inaugurated the cold war against the Soviet Union by issuing the Truman Doctrine of March 12, 1947. That doctrine went way beyond opposition to Communism to justify American suppression of nationalist revolutions against control by foreign corporations. Truman wrote: "I believe it must be the policy of the United States to support free peoples who are resisting attempted subjugation by armed minorities or by outside pressure."

Everything depended on who defined and how they defined the meaning of "free peoples," "armed minorities" and "outside pressure." "Armed minorities" could mean Communist-led guerrillas, or it could mean nationalists wanting to determine their own country's destiny. "Free peoples" could mean a country with free elections or it could mean a dictatorship that granted freedom to American corporations to exploit the people. The Truman assumption, factually incorrect, was that all revolutions against governments in the American sphere of influence were Communist-inspired.

D. F. Fleming, professor of international relations at Vanderbilt University, former adviser to the atomic energy section of the State Department, and author of *The Cold War and Its Origins,* described the long range consequences of the Truman Doctrine. "First, it automatically put us in the business of playing God to all the less fortunate peoples" by interfering "to prevent social revolution. This was *Pax Americana.* Second, by proscribing Communism and implicitly proclaiming the encirclement of the Soviet Union, the doctrine launched the world into a global power-ideological struggle and a vast arms race. . . . Third, the doctrine relegated the United Nations to near impotence by destroying the key assumption on which it was built; . . . that the United States and the Soviet Union could cooperate in leading the new United Nations. Instead the Truman Doctrine decreed that Communism was synonymous with 'terror and oppression' and soon we were being taught, endlessly and monotonously, that the ruined and exhausted Soviet peoples were out to conquer the world."[1]

Over the years since 1947 the C.I.A., American troops, and troops of puppet governments trained by the United States invaded Guatemala, the Dominican Republic, Lebanon, Korea, Vietnam, and other countries to quell revolts or install governments friendly to American interests. Only in Vietnam was there an immediate defeat. In order to suppress revolutions, American leaders justified intervention overseas as defending its security or human freedom from Communism. They also used Army Special Forces to train American troops and armies of other countries to "kill social dissenters" abroad. Schools in the United States trained foreign troops in counterinsurgency. A jungle warfare school in Panama, and other schools in Okinawa and Germany also trained foreign troops to suppress revolution. Two police academies, one in Panama and one in Washington, trained foreign police forces. Other programs, including those sponsored by the C.I.A., were created for the same purpose.[2]

It is difficult to tell whether top American leaders actually believed the Soviet Union planned to conquer the world or whether this idea was created to permit the military-industrial complex to build a huge American sphere of influence. There is no evidence that the Soviets ever intended to invade Western Europe or conquer other countries. Many scholars believe such a danger never existed.

Marxist-Leninist theory held that war was inevitable. But it would be waged between capitalist nations or by capitalist countries against socialist states. There is nothing in Leninist theory that calls for the military aggression of Communist against capitalist countries. Rather, Communist theory and strategy have clearly attempted to avoid war with the capitalist world. This policy has been demonstrated by the Soviet policy of coexistence. Communist theory does provide for giving military aid to revolutionaries engaged in "wars of national liberation." However, Lenin believed that revolution could not be imported and could occur only as a result of the internal disintegration of capitalist society and the internal revolt of the people who lived in it.

Communist theory and practice are hostile to capitalism. But, wrote Fred Warner Neal, professor of government at the Claremont Graduate School and University Center in Claremont, California, "there was nothing calling for initiation of military action by Moscow. To make up for this lack, there has arisen a body of wholly false quotations attributed to Lenin, Stalin, and others in which they carefully explained that all Russians were waiting for was for the West to let down its guard."[3]

For example, Governor Nelson Rockefeller was given the following item, attributed to Lenin, for use in his 1960 campaign: "Our immutable aim, after all, is world conquest . . . " Professor Neal also noted "another bit of apocrypha" that has "Dimitry Manuilsky, onetime head of the Comintern, saying that Soviet talk of peace is merely a trick to lull the capitalist nations and that 'as soon as their guard is down, we smash them with our clenched fist.' "[4]

The fear of the Soviet Union has been imbedded or "institutionalized" in the minds of the American people not only by events, but through various myths, ideas, or slogans. They have made it difficult for us to understand the Soviet Union in any way other than untrustworthy, aggressive, and warlike.

An examination of such myths or slogans may be helpful in giving a new perspective to American-Soviet relations. One of these ideas was coined by Nikita Khrushchev, a former Soviet leader, in his statement, "We will bury you." That statement has been used to suggest that the Soviet Union intends militarily to defeat or destroy the United States. It is a kind of colloquial phrase that could as easily have been translated: "We will triumph over you." It should not be taken literally or understood as a threat of military violence. Rather, it means that the future will prove the validity and triumph of Soviet ideas. Is Khrushchev's statement any different from Ronald Reagan's assertion that the Soviet Union will end up "on the ash heap of history?" Is one statement any less threatening than the other?

The question of intention to bury or triumph over can be seen in at least two quite different ways. One is by political analysis. From the Soviet perspective the world, however slowly, is moving away from capitalism. No nation in Africa has the capital or resources to maintain modern capitalism, except possibly South Africa. There are none in South America. Only Japan in Asia and Germany in Europe have the potential, but even they can develop them only with the assistance of the United States.

"Capitalism in Western Europe," according to a recent review, "is changing rapidly. In some countries state-owned companies amount to nearly half of the industrial sector, including control of key industries. European governments now have a direct ownership in over half of Europe's fifty largest companies."[5] None of this implies a movement towards Communism or rigid government control. It does, however, signify movement away from traditional private enterprise.

A second way of interpreting the intention to bury is by military action. Charles Rivers in the July 1983 *U.S. Farm News* wrote: "While the Soviet Union has never invaded our country, we have invaded the Soviet Union. While the Soviet Union has never attempted to overthrow our government, we did try to overthrow the Soviet government by force and violence. While the Soviet Union has never blockaded us, we did blockade the Soviet Union when it was in shambles following World War I, . . . thus denying them the food and medicine they desperately needed."

General Maxwell Taylor, former chairman of the Joint Chiefs of Staff, rejected the idea that the Soviet Union was planning war against the United States. He said Soviet forces are defensively oriented. They "have conventional forces in close proximity to virtually all their national interests that may require defense. Thus they would have no reason to resort to nuclear weapons for defense. Second, from their World War II experience, their leaders know how devastating conventional war can be. They also know that nuclear war would be many times more destructive, that they would lose in a few hours more than they lost in four years fighting the Germans. Third, they could not afford to fight or even win a strategic war with the United States. In so doing they would so paralyze the nation as to make it easy prey to nearby neighbors — wolves ready to take advantage of a stricken bear. Such enemies would include Chinese, Afghans, Turks, Germans and Poles *beyond* Soviet borders and non-Russians *within*."[6]

Has the Soviet Union been attempting gradually to take over the world? The answer is clearly No! Soviet armed forces or military missions were once in Egypt, Somalia, the Sudan, and China. They left when asked to leave and are in none of those places today. Instead, an American military presence has been established in Egypt, Somalia, and the Sudan. The Soviet Union has the allegiance of no more than nineteen nations, whereas the *Des Moines Register* (March 27, 1981) reported that the United States had military trainers and technicians in fifty-three countries.

Vice Admiral M. Staser Holcomb, former director of Navy program planning, in discussing Soviet naval forces, stated: " . . . the total capability of the Soviet force of amphibious ships is to land 12,000 naval infantrymen under benign conditions; that is, to land them at a pier or shoreline where nobody is opposing them. It is not amphibious assault capability. Our sixty-six [amphibious] ships represent the ability to punch in with a division. That is a different ballgame altogether." The *Defense Monitor,* published by the Center for Defense Information and staffed by retired Pentagon officers, concludes that the Soviets do not have "powerful military forces for long-range intervention in other countries."[8]

A second myth is that the Soviet Union is the source of conflict and evil in the world. President Reagan in his March 1983 speech to the National Association of Evangelicals referred to the Soviet Union as "the focus of evil in the modern world." He called it "an evil empire" and American-Soviet rivalry a "struggle between right and wrong, good and evil."

We cannot, however, speak of huge conglomerates of power as moral or immoral in the same way as one speaks of individuals. Does the fact that the Soviets have not used nuclear weapons on any cities make them more moral than the United States, which first developed and then exploded atomic bombs over two Japanese cities and killed thousands of civilians?

The claim that the Soviet Union is an evil empire is based on such actions as armed intervention in Hungary, Czechoslovakia, and Afghanistan in order to guarantee that regimes responsive to Soviet policies would stay in control of those nations. The United States, however, has a longer and more extensive history of armed intervention in such places as Nicaragua, Mexico, Guatemala, the Dominican Republic, El Salvador, Vietnam, and Grenada to seek or maintain control over their governments. Americans also use the C.I.A. to overthrow foreign governments, as it did in Chile in 1973. The United States today is engaged in the military occupation of Honduras in order to control the Central American region. The lesson to be learned from this is that all "great powers" operate in much the same way. They abide by agreements not to intervene in other countries, such as they signed in accepting the United Nations Charter, only when they deem it in their interest to do so. They violate them when they think their interests require the exercise of military power. The only way one can speak of one great power as evil and the other as good is by concealing American interventions and focusing only on Soviet actions.

Our leaders often blame the Soviet Union for the failure of American policies in other countries. The Soviets are said to be responsible for all the unrest that is going on. "If they weren't engaged in the game of dominoes, there wouldn't be any hotspots in the world,"[9] according to Mr. Reagan. This is another misreading of history. The Soviet Union had little to do with such "hotspots" as the Argentine invasion of the Falklands or the British war against Argentina. It was the C.I.A. and the United States, not the Soviets, that installed the Shah in Iran, against whom there was an Islamic revolt led by Ayatollah Khomeini. It was American marines that put the dictator Somoza in power in Nicaragua, against whom a nationalist revolution was fought and won in 1979. It was the C.I.A. that overthrew the elected democratic government of Guatemala after the latter had expropriated 160,000 uncultivated acres of land belonging to the United Fruit Company. The Soviet Union had nothing to do with the expropriation or with the nonviolent revolution that earlier had unseated Ubico, an American-backed dictator. The current guerrilla warfare in Guatemala is against right-wing oppressive regimes installed by the United States.

These illustrations do not exhaust the evidence of "hotspots" in which the Soviets were not involved.

A third myth the Pentagon and various American Presidents have used is that it is only American military superiority that has prevented Soviet aggression. Fred Warner Neal, referring to the period after the development of the Soviet *sputniki,* wrote: "According to American cold war ideology, Soviet military aggression had been restrained only by our superior military strength. Now that it wasn't so superior any more, the Soviets should have attacked, and, truth to tell, Washington was hard pressed to say why they didn't."[10]

Neither did the Soviet Union engage in any aggression when the United States bogged down in a long, losing war in Vietnam. During the period when many spoke of Soviet superiority and attacked Gerald Ford for letting us become number two, the Soviets did not attack. Of course, the United States was not number two. America's leaders cannot have it both ways. They cannot claim Soviet military superiority in order to get larger military appropriations and at the same time claim that it is American superiority that keeps the Soviets from aggression. If the answer is that it is nuclear weapons that deterred the Soviets, we might well ask why it is necessary to have superiority at all. Why should the United States pour billions into NATO and keep hundreds of thousands of troops in Western Europe, Japan, and other countries. It is not necessary to have superiority, except as part of the myth that only superiority prevents aggression.

One of the allegations made against the Soviets, a myth many Americans accept, is the idea that "you can't trust the Russians." This myth is not altogether false. It should be evident from the long history of international relations that all nations are untrustworthy. They do not keep promises the way individuals do. By invading Grenada, the United States broke at least two treaties, the United Nations Charter and an agreement with the Organization of American States. It would be surprising if the Soviets had not also broken treaties. However, Kosta Tsipis, the associate director of the Program in Science and Technology for International Security at the Massachusetts Institute of Technology, wrote in the April 1982 *Bulletin of the Atomic Scientists* that "history and the diplomatic record show that the Soviet Union has never broken or abrogated a treaty."

It is a little known fact that the United States and the Soviet

Union established in the early 1970s a standing consultative commission to discuss complaints of violations of provisions in their mutual arms control treaties. All complaints thus far have referred to minor violations that on investigation have either been found to be false or have been rectified to the satisfaction of the other nation. As William Sloane Coffin points out, when it comes to making deals that are in our interest, such as the selling of grain, we trust the Russians.

Another widely believed myth says, "You can't negotiate with the Soviets." Edward Teller in the November 1982 *Readers Digest* wrote: "We have negotiated for twenty-five years, and the results are readily visible. Why would a totalitarian empire that depends on military force to maintain its power voluntarily disarm itself!" The truth is that neither the United States nor the Soviet Union has used nuclear weapons to maintain order within its own or satellite countries. Teller is mistaken when he asserts that disarmament deprives nations of police or other forces necessary to maintain order. The treaties for complete disarmament proposed in the 1950s and 1960s provided for the equivalent of a national or state militia such as the National Guard to maintain internal order. Those militia could be armed for riot control, but not with offensive weapons such as bombers.

Teller is also wrong in saying that "you can't negotiate with the Soviets." In the period since World War II the United States and the Soviet Union have negotiated a number of treaties. They include the following: (1) An Antarctica treaty banning armaments in that continent; (2) the ABM treaty limiting antiballistic missile systems; (3) an agreement on verification (technically Article XII of the ABM treaty), which provides for national technical means of verification such as satellites and for noninterference with such means, and which prohibits deliberate concealment methods; (4) a treaty providing for a standing consultative commission to consider questions of compliance with arms control treaties; (5) an Accident Measures Agreement relating to the prevention of nuclear war and a Direct Communications Link or Hot Line Agreement: (6) a Limited Test Ban Treaty; (7) the Nonproliferation Treaty; and (8) the SALT II Treaty, which has been ratified by the Soviet Union but not the United States. In addition, two treaties have been negotiated and signed prior to Reagan's election. Reagan has refused to submit them to the Senate for ratification. These are an agreement to prohibit tests of nuclear weapons with an explosive force of more than 150 kilotons, and another that provides for information exchange and on-site inspection of peaceful uses of nuclear explosives.

These and other agreements reveal that it is not only possible to negotiate with the Russians, but that the United States has refused to ratify three treaties that both it and the Soviet Union negotiated and signed.

A sixth myth of long standing is that any negotiation with the Soviet Union must be from "a position of strength." This implies that if the United States is much stronger than the Soviet Union, it can drive a hard bargain and negotiate a treaty to its advantage. The history of negotiations with the Soviet Union and other great powers is that they cannot be intimidated into signing treaties contrary to their national interest. The fallacy in the myth of negotiating from strength is this: weak nations that increase their strength are likely to violate or abrogate a treaty they were coerced into signing. Treaties that last must respect the national interest of all parties to the treaty. Hence they do not depend on strength.

Still another allegation charges that the Soviet Union is behind international terrorism. The word "terrorist" is, of course, a propaganda term. American mercenaries, which the C.I.A. employs to interfere in countries such as Nicaragua, are called "freedom fighters," although they are drawn from the former dictator's National Guard. But those Nicaraguans who may suffer injury and death at their hands call them "terrorists." A terrorist is someone on the other side who, through acts of violence, creates fear. Even if identical acts are performed by your side, those acts are not called terrorist. Unfortunately, both super powers have supported so-called friendly governments who engage in activity that can with some justification be called terrorist. The Soviets frequently white-wash these terrible deeds. At the same time our media describes the wanton violence of the powerful as "defense," but they reserve the term "terrorists" to label the violence employed on behalf of the poor.

Not all of the fear Americans have of the Russians comes from Soviet behavior, or the rhetoric of Presidents and defense secretaries. Much of it comes from the mere fact that there are only two great powers, and that they are heavily armed and ideological rivals. This means that those in the armed forces and hence their families and friends are indoctrinated at many levels to believe the worst of the enemy. Many of the false pictures of the Soviets come right out of the armed forces. Films, lectures, misinformation, one-sided presentations with no opportunity for dissent or correction, all play their part. Military officers impersonate Soviet personnel to provide supposedly authentic information or to taunt the audience.

The Associated Press in December 1983 reported that navy intelligence officers pretending to be Russians "portray Soviet sailors boasting of their dedication, ridiculing American attitudes, and giving first-person accounts of how Communists view the world. . . . On stage, an officer in a Soviet uniform shouts in a thick Russian accent, villifying decadent America as a 'society . . . in its death throes.' United States sailors are the audience." The press account said: "Since March a five-member team headed by the intelligence training center commander, Capt. Paul Laska, has presented the show to fifteen thousand people at nineteen Navy bases from Bermuda to Hawaii."[11]

Much of the fear of an enemy is irrational, a result of dehumanization. Some of it is real because preparation for war brutalizes those on both sides. Americans, however, must deal with their own fears, must stop dehumanizing other people, and must encourage both Russians and themselves to recognize that we have an overarching common nuclear enemy. It is an integral part of the military institution and political system that make war possible.

5

THE ARM'S RACE: WHO'S AHEAD?

Pam Solo

The bomb was born in secrecy. It was born in the heat of war with Hitler's Germany. Fears that Hitler was close to developing an atomic bomb were somewhat justified. Nuclear fission was first discovered in Berlin in 1938. Scientists throughout the world knew the potential for creating it. In the United States, Britain, the Soviet Union, and perhaps elsewhere, scientists were trying to create chain reactions as early as 1940. The realization that Hitler might beat the Allies to the creation of the atomic bomb fueled and crystallized the most intensive collaboration between the military and scientists in the history of the country. It was in this military and political context that people dedicated themselves to the creation of the most horrible technology in all of human history—nuclear weapons.

Robert J. Oppenheimer, the charismatic and brilliant head of the Manhattan project (the original bomb project), recounts the day the bomb was dropped on Hiroshima. In his papers and memoirs he recalls a "celebration" at Los Alamos after the first use of nuclear weapons in Japan. He went over to the party half-heartedly. As he approached the building, he saw a usually "cool-headed young scientist vomiting in the bushes." "The reaction has begun," Oppenheimer thought to himself.

This sense of dread and remorse grew in Oppenheimer. It led to his famous phrase concerning the bomb, "Physicists have known sin." Oppenheimer knew, as did Einstein and others, the full impact of the splitting of the atom. While some in the Manhattan project urged that the bomb not be dropped on population centers, the technological imperative was driving the political machinery ahead. As President Truman said, "We found the bomb and we used it." After the bombings of Nagasaki and Hiroshima, Oppenheimer argued that the technical and scientific information be quickly shared in an international forum so as to promote its control. Instead, the United States launched a massive effort to build a nationwide nuclear weapons production, research, and testing complex.

In addition to assisting the war effort against Hitler, the handful of scientists, which grew to a force of some 6,000 at Los Alamos, New Mexico, were driven by another dynamic. They were racing to achieve a technological accomplishment they knew would revolutionize science. The mysteries of the earth were being unfolded in their work. Abundant power was in their hands. Their work was technically and professionally engaging. They were caught in the "technological sweetness" of the challenge. The technological imperative behind the arms race was given birth out of this marriage between the military and scientific communities.

Those who participated in the Manhattan project knew that they were approaching the very edge of history. Aware of the awesome power they were about to unleash, they named the first test "Trinity." No one knew or sure how this first test would go. Scientists acknowledged that they even suspected the chain reaction would be uncontrollable. Their doubts and uncertainties did not stop the test. Trinity was a 'success.' The first words that came to Oppenheimer at the Trinity site were from the Bhagavad Gita:

> If the radiance of a thousand suns
> Were to burst at once into the sky,
> That would be like the splendour of the Mighty One.
> I am become Death,
> The shatterer of worlds.

The power, the domination of the secrets of the universe, the control of the most awesome power known in all of human history have driven the arms race forward. In this sense we see the ultimate moral and spiritual challenge presented by the nuclear arms race. If such bombs are ever used, human beings will have taken to themselves the authority to end all of God's creation once and for all. To prepare for their use is no less idolatrous.

The British and the Americans were conducting atomic projects in great secrecy, without informing the Soviet Union—then our ally. This drive for the ultimate military power was not being pursued only in the United States. Soviet work on the bomb had begun in earnest in 1942. The race had begun. Cold war politics started very early on, stimulated in part by the politics of the bomb itself.

David Halloway in *The Soviet Union and the Arms Race* writes that on July 24, 1945 (days after the Trinity test) President

Truman approached Stalin after the formal session and mentioned to him that "we had a new weapon of unusual destructive force." Truman later wrote that Stalin replied that he was "glad to hear of it and hoped we would make good use of it against the Japanese." Truman and Churchill (who was standing nearby) were convinced that Stalin had not grasped what the President was referring to. They were mistaken, for by the time of the Potsdam conference, the Soviet Union had a full scale bomb project underway, a project Stalin did not reveal to Truman and Churchill.

If Stalin had been told earlier about the bomb, his postwar attitude might not have been any different. However, Holloway speculates, "Western secrecy contributed to Soviet suspicion and spurred the Soviet Union to develop its own bomb." Mutual suspicion and secrecy took root and have been growing ever since.

At the end of the Second World War the Soviet Union faced not only an advanced Western bomb but backwardness in other military technologies such as long range missiles and radar. The war devastated them economically and physically. They lost twenty million of their people. In spite of this, by the summer of 1946 the Soviet Union had put in motion the mechanisms for its own counterpart to the American weapons program. The late 1940s and early 1950s brought Soviet advances in missile technology and warhead developments. On August 29, 1949, the Soviet Union tested its first nuclear weapon.

While Washington knew of the Soviet weapons program, it did not expect the Russians to have the bomb until 1950. This early success shocked governmental leaders and led to Truman's decision to accelerate the American program on thermonuclear weapons. Oppenheimer once again argued strongly against the effort. "The extreme dangers . . . inherent in the proposal wholly outweigh any military advantage that could come from this development.

Dr. Edward Teller led the scientific charge to develop these weapons. The decision was made to move up to the next level of technological sophistication. The political, academic, military, and industrial machinery for the arms race was set in motion. These social and political institutions are elements in the nuclear trap we have laid for ourselves. Each must also, therefore, be addressed in our search for a way out of the trap.

The history of the arms race is one of action and reaction. It was born in secrecy and paranoia, in the heat of war; it began in the early stages of Cold War politics. The history of the arms race is a history of miscalculation, misperception, lack of communication, the meeting of one technical innovation by another. It is a history of two giant nations competing for influence around the world. The politics of the arms race was set in Yalta with the division of Europe by the two superpowers into spheres of influence. Now this bipolar world between East and West is being extended into competition for influence, each superpower projecting its military muscle on behalf of "vital interests" into regions of the world struggling for their own economic development and national identity.

Forty years later the world, particularly the Third World, has become the arena in which the United States and the Soviet Union play their deadly game of nuclear chicken. There are other players. Great Britain, China, and France are all major nuclear powers. Other nations thought to have the bomb or be developing it are Israel, South Africa, Argentina, India, and Pakistan. The U.S. Department of Energy estimates that by 1985 thirty-five countries will have nuclear weapons.

It has taken nearly four decades of the arms race—relatively unrestrained—to bring us to this moment in history. Now we are faced with a growing nuclear threat from a proliferation of nuclear weapons to several nations. Technological innovations by the superpowers combined with increased East-West hostility and regional wars in the Middle East, Central America, and elsewhere threaten to spin out of our control. Localized conflicts threaten to become the occasions for American-Soviet conflict and the use of nuclear weapons.

The analogy of the high school biology experiment is an apt description of our dilemma. Students were asked to drop a live frog into a beaker of boiling water. Hitting the hot water, the frog immediately jumped out and saved his life. Taking the same frog, students were asked to put the frog in a beaker of cold water and slowly bring the water to a boil. The frog adapted in increments, allowing itself to be boiled to death. Since the late 1940s we have been adapting in increments to the nuclear threat—East and West. We still have time before we allow ourselves to make the last "adaptation" . . . but there is not much time.

Around 1979 a resurgence of a political and military philosophy came center stage in the midst of the SALT II debate, the Soviet invasion of Afghanistan, and later the Iranian hostage crisis. The banner became "peace through strength." Major campaigns and coalitions were built by groups like the Moral Majority, the American Conservative Union, the Heritage Foundation, Phyllis Schlafly's Eagle Forum, and others.

The arguments of the proponents of the "peace through

strength" philosophy go something like this: The Soviets are ahead of the United States militarily. The United States has for a decade let "military modernization" give way to domestic social concerns and the wrongheadedness of "liberal" politicians. The United States lost its will after defeat in Vietnam. We are losing influence and respect around the world because we are unwilling to use our military strength in defense of our national interests. We used to be number one, but even little countries like Iran can push us around. We must overcome this "Viet Nam syndrome" and overcome our fear of using our military might to defend democracy and freedom, protect our "vital interests," and defeat Communism. The bomb is a "gift from God" [direct quote from Schlafly]. Nuclear deterrence has worked. Therefore, we should trust it to work in the future. We must build new nuclear weapons to "catch up" to the Russians.

This litany only slightly caricatures the arguments of those who advocate increased and continued reliance on nuclear weapons as the keystone of our security policy. Let's look at these assertions and some of the arguments against them.

Deterrence has been the centerpiece of the nuclear arms race since the day nuclear weapons could be delivered from Soviet soil to ours and ours to theirs. Deterrence is built on the belief that the other side will be deterred from using its nuclear weapons if using them invites a retaliatory strike of equal devastation. The balance of terror has been given the official military policy name of Mutual Assured Destruction or MAD.

An ICBM (intercontinental ballistic missile) can deliver nuclear weapons to the United States or the Soviet Union within thirty minutes. Long-range bombers and submarine-launched missiles have varying delivery times, depending on their location. The exact number of nuclear warheads is probably not known. The United Nations estimates the total to be in excess of forty thousand. Other prominent researchers such as SIPRI (Stockholm International Peace Research Institute) put the number at around fifty thousand today and well over sixty thousand by the early 1990s. The explosive force of these warheads ranges from one hundred tons up to the equivalent of twenty million tons of chemical high explosives. The total strength of present nuclear arsenals is estimated to be equal to about one million Hiroshima-sized bombs, or thirteen million tons of TNT, more than three tons for every man, woman, and child on earth.

The superpowers have enough deliverable nuclear warheads to destroy everyone on the earth several times over. However, even if one accepts the idea of deterrence, there is a strong argument for sufficiency being a measure of the superpowers' nuclear stockpiles. We can only die once.

Deterrence implies an "acceptable number of casualties" one is willing to sustain as one tries to deliver a crippling blow to one's adversary. This balance of terror has become the context in which all international discourse has taken place since the early 1950s. Security is based on our willingness to launch nuclear weapons that could ignite the final conflagration and result in mutual assured suicide. The creation of fear and unpredictability becomes the cornerstone for a "national security" policy. In fact, stability, security, and peace are concepts totally antithetical to the instability, insecurity, and confrontation fueled by the nuclear arms race itself.

Deterrence is described as a defensive military policy. The fact is that nuclear war is offensive. There can be no defense against a missile that can't be recalled. The one who launches first and hits with the greatest number of its nuclear weapons has — from the military's point of view — the advantage. Of course, in nuclear war there can be no advantage because of the destruction created by even a limited use of nuclear weapons.

Nuclear weapons have no value in the military sense if one is not willing to threaten their use and to use them. Politicians and military planners refer to keeping a "credible deterrent." By this they mean not only a sufficient number of deliverable nuclear weapons, but also a military posture and policy that convinces the adversary that their use is thinkable. Advocates of deterrence argue that only under these conditions can peace and détente be built and sustained between the superpowers.

However, deterrence can fail. The margin of error is steadily decreasing with greater American-Soviet hostility combined with new technological developments.

There seems to be a near total denial or ignorance of the effects of nuclear weapons. Decision makers would do well to read a special edition of the Swedish Academy of Sciences Journal *Ambio,* published in 1982, entitled *Nuclear War: The Aftermath.* It describes what would happen if less than half the nuclear warheads were exploded: "More than half the 1.3 billion people living in the northern hemisphere are killed at once, 350 million are seriously wounded, and many of the 20 million 'survivors' die later on of radiation injuries or epidemics. Smoke, soot, gravel, and dust are pumped into the atmosphere, and the sky is dark even during the day for weeks and weeks, even perhaps for months. Agriculture in the northern hemisphere is wiped out, food supplies break down, and more people — particularly in the Third World — die from starvation than from the immediate and secondary effects of the weapons."

Numerous studies are available that go into great detail. Their reading should be required for anyone running for public office.

Counterforce has helped to undermine the already fragile "stability" of deterrence. This strategy has escalated the danger of nuclear war. With the development of first-strike weapons we now have the technology that may tempt the first use of nuclear weapons in a superpower conflict. The Soviets have on their drawing boards weapons that parallel the MX, Trident II, and Pershing II missiles . . . all first-strike weapons. First-strike weapons are fast and highly accurate weapons that may seduce military planners into attempting a preemptive strike, hoping to cripple the other side by reducing their ability to launch a retaliatory blow. This threat of a disarming first strike is the most destabilizing aspect of the new generation of nuclear weapons.

President Carter formalized this new first-strike military policy in Presidential Directive 59. President Reagan moved with dispatch to produce an unprecedented number of new weapons, an estimated twenty thousand nuclear warheads within a decade. Some of these will replace existing weapons. Others will add to the overall total. Although the policy of fighting and winning nuclear wars began in the Carter administration, Reagan's administration demonstrated a greater willingness to use nuclear weapons for political gain in global conflicts. Reagan signed another directive formalizing his administration's military doctrine, NSDD 32. This doctrine arrived at a strategy for fighting prolonged conventional war, decided on geographic and political priorities, and produced a strategy for protracted nuclear war if deterrence failed (*New York Times,* January 15, 1984). The *Times* further reported that Reagan's military doctrine emphasized that "the nuclear triad of intercontinental ballistic missiles, submarine-launched ballistic missiles, and aircraft carrying nuclear bombs must be as invulnerable as possible."[11] More important, it called for "communications that would survive a nuclear attack and permit the President and his advisers to fight a prolonged war."

Another claim of the peace through strength (PTS) proponents is that the "Soviets are ahead. The United States needs to modernize its nuclear weapons and restore parity with the Russians." It is clear that "parity" should be translated "superiority." Being essentially equal with Soviet nuclear forces is being "behind." In fact, the United States is *not* behind the Russians. We have led the arms race at almost every stage with technological advances, with the Soviets following with comparable developments.

The Soviets have opted to base most of their nuclear warheads on land. The United States developed a Triad system, stationing nuclear weapons at sea, on long range bombers, and on ICBMs. A greater proportion of American missiles are based at sea on invulnerable submarines. The Soviets lead in the number of missiles, the lifting power of the missiles, and the overall explosive force deliverable by those missiles. Numerically they have more submarines, but they are significantly inferior to those of the United States. In addition to having a superior and invulnerable submarine force, the United States is ahead in the number of long-range bombers and in cruise missile technology, not to mention the speed and accuracy of its missiles. Americans have "MIRVed" more of their missiles. "MIRVing" means fixing a number of independently targetable warheads on one missile. We have more deliverable warheads than does the Soviet Union. The Soviet Union is said to be able to deliver around six thousand warheads, the United States ten thousand.

Table 1. U.S. and Soviet strategic nuclear weapon delivery capability

U.S.A.			U.S.S.R.		
Delivery vehicle		No. of warheads	Delivery vehicle		No. of warheads
ICBMs:	1,051	2,151	ICBMs:	1,398	5,678
SLBMs:	644	4,960	SLBMs:	937	2,813
Bombers:	316	2,570	Bombers:	145	290
Total:	**2,011**	**9,681**	**Total:**	**2,480**	**8,781**

Compiled by the Stockholm International Peace Research Institute.

In addition to these long-range strategic weapons the Soviet Union and the United States have tactical, short-range, battlefield nuclear weapons. These include nuclear shells for tanks. Another class of nuclear weapons is the so-called intermediate range nuclear force (INF). The weapons being deployed in Europe fall into this category. Many experts feel these weapons should be included in the strategic category because of their accuracy, range, and speed of delivery. The Soviets feel these weapons represent a threat to them parallel to that of long-range weapons because they can reach strategic targets in the U.S.S.R.

The Soviets have deployed 370 SS-20s, two-thirds of which are directed toward Western Europe, and the remainder at China. A portion of those aimed at Western Europe can be used against the

Table 2. World nuclear weapon stockpiles

		1951	1955	1960	1965	1967	1970	1975	1980	1982
U.S.A.	a	400	1,050	3,375	21,338	25,770	28,390	31,802	30,523	30,420
	b	..	..	..	..	..	28,390	31,802	30523	30,420
	c	1,000	2,000	20,000	31,800	32,000	27,000	28,000	26,000	26,000
	d									"Low tens of thousands"
	e									30,000
	f									31,200
U.S.S.R.	a	6	340	2,220	4,681	6,343	7,870	11,370	15,170	15,670
	b	..	..	..	..	..	7,870	11,570	15,670	17,470
	e									25,000
	f									17,400
	g									17,800 – 22,800
China	a	..	..	..	2	9	54	330	730	920
	b	..	..	..	..	..	54	332	740	942
France	a	..	..	1	27	60	110	330	625	720
	b	..	..	..	..	..	460	540	600	640
	h									1,700
Total										
(lowest –		408 –	1,410 –	5,783 –	26,468 –	32,661 –	35,494 –	40,570 –	43,125 –	43,950 –
highest figures)		1,008	2,360	22,408	36,930	38,891	36,908	44,644	48,278	59,562

Sources: a. 'Military record of CBR/atomic happenings', *Aviation Studies Atlantic* (London), January 1982.
   b. 'Military record of CBR/atomic happenings', *Aviation Studies Atlantic* (London), September 1982.
   c. Arkin, W. M., Cochran, T. B. and Hoenig, M. M., 'The U.S. nuclear stockpile', *Arms Control Today*, 12, No. 4 (April, 1982).
   d. Office of Assistant Secretary of Defense (Public Affairs), News Release, June 1, 1982; Department of State handout (n.d.).
   e. 'Pentagon official' cited by Ed Scherr, *USIA Diplomatic Correspondent*, December 12, 1982.
   f. Sivard, R. L., *World Military and Social Expenditures* 1982.
   g. *Defense Monitor* (Center for Defense Information), 11, No. 1 (World Priorities, Leesburg, Va., 1982).
   h. Gallagher, J., *Nuclear Stocktaking: A Count of Britain's Warheads*, Bailrigg Paper on International Security No. 5 (University of Lancaster), 1982.
   Compiled by the Stockholm International Peace Research Institute.

Middle East, the Far East, and Southeast Asia. The SS-20 replaced an older missile and has a solid fuel rocket, enabling it to be launched quickly. The older rockets required a couple of hours for fueling before launch. The SS-20 can be reloaded after several hours. Its mobility is limited. The SS-20 represents a modernization of Soviet technology, which has lagged far behind that of the United States. The Soviets took a long time to recognize why this advancement might be viewed with alarm in the West. It did represent an increased capacity and sophistication, but certainly not beyond established Western capacities.

On the other hand, in 1979 NATO and the United States proposed the deployment of 572 new INF missiles. These are known as the Eurostrategic missiles, or Ground-Launched Cruise (GLCMs) and Pershing II missiles. The Pershing II will be deployed in West Germany, the GLCMs in Britain, Italy, Belgium, and the Netherlands. These new missiles were proposed by West German Chancellor Helmut Schmidt. Schmidt's concern was that in the event of a Soviet invasion of Western Europe the United States would not be willing to flex its nuclear muscle. We would have to launch weapons from the continental United States, and that would invite a Soviet response. The Americans, thought Schmidt, would not trade Chicago for Hamburg. Europe needed to "couple" its security with America's. Having new American weapons capable of reaching the Soviet Union would insure American involvement. The missiles had from the beginning more political than military significance. However, they were sold to the American taxpayer and the European public as a necessary counter to the modernized Soviet SS-20.

The American Cruise and Pershing II represent a technological escalation of the arms race. The Pershing has a range and accuracy that will enable it to reach strategic targets within the Soviet Union in twelve minutes. The Cruise missile has precision guidance that allows it to fly low to the ground, constantly adjusting its course by a computer read-out of the terrain. While it is slow flying, it is also destabilizing because it flies under radar and is therefore undetectable. The Soviets may respond by going on "launch on warning," i.e., computers will launch a nuclear response at the first apparent indication of Western missiles—even if it is only a flock of geese or a computer chip failure.

The Soviets insist that their modernization is not threatening. They argue that their intermediate range forces are a counter to American missiles and to the independent nuclear forces of the British and French. Both sides argue for equality and parity, but

Table 3. Long-range theatre nuclear missiles

Country	Missile designation	Year first deployed	Range (km)	CEP (m)	Warhead(s)	Inventory[1] A	B	Programme status
U.S.S.R.	SS-4 Sandal	1959	1,800	2,400	1 × Mt	232	..	Phasing out
	SS-5 Skean	1961	3,500	1,200	1 × Mt	16	..	Phasing out
	SS-20	1976/77	5,000	400	1 × 150-kt MIRV	333	..	Deployment rate approximately 50 per year
	SS-N-5 Serb	1963	1,200	n.a.	1 × ?[2]; 1 × Mt	30	18	3 each on Golf II submarines, 6 of which have been deployed in the Baltic since 1976
U.S.A.	Pershing II	1983	1,800	40	1 × ? (low-kt)	0		108 launchers to be deployed by 1985
	GLCM	1983	2,500	50	1 × ?[3]	0		464 missiles to be deployed by 1988
U.K.	Polaris A-3	1967	4,600	800	3 × 200-kt MRV	64		On 4 SSBNs, being replaced by the Chevaline system[4]
	Trident II (D-5)[5]	(1990s)	10,000	250	8 × 355-kt MIRV	0		Replacing the Polaris/Chevaline system from the 1990s, with 64 launchers on 4 submarines
France	SSBS S-3	1980	3,000	n.a.	1 × 1-Mt	18		On 5 SSBNs
	MSBS M-20	1977	3,000	n.a.	1 × 1-Mt	80		On the 6th SSBN; total programme, including retrofits: 96 (by 1992)
	MSBS M-4	(1985)	4,000	n.a.	6 × 150-kt MRV	0		

Compiled by the Stockholm International Peace Research Institute.

[1] A: U.S. figures, from *Soviet Military Power* (Washington, DC, U.S. Government Printing Office. March 1983). B: The Soviet Union released figures for missiles deployed at the end of 1981, but had not published updated figures by the turn of the year 1982/83. Two-thirds of the SS-4s, SS-5s and SS-20s are estimated to be within striking range of Europe.

[2] Some SS-20 missiles are equipped with a single warhead and may therefore have intercontinental range.

[3] The W.84 warhead, with a selectable yield.

[4] Probably with three warheads (MRV), each of 50 kt, have also been indicated.

[5] Range and yield are based on the likely U.S. choice of warheads. Since the U.K. will supply its own charges, it may choose force specifications that differ from those of the U.S.A.

neither side can agree on which weapons are part of the equation. For example, bomber forces and submarines off the coast of the European continent are part of this controversy.

There are other weapons now on the drawing boards for both the Soviets and the United States. Laser, particle beams, and an antisattelite arms race in space threaten to make the 1990s and the early part of the next century even more precarious — assuming we make it through the rest of the decade.

Weapons of mass annhilation have been the primary focus thus far. The nuclear arms race has made world security fragile, to say the least. And yet it should be said that nuclear weapons represent only a small part of the arms race. They are the smallest percentage of military budgets. World military expenditures will reach eight hundred billion in 1984. "The superpowers account for 50 percent of this, 70 percent of international weapons exports, 80 percent of world expenditures on military research and development, and they possess 95 percent of all nuclear weapons in the world," according to Maj. Britt Theorin, Swedish ambassador to the Geneva disarmament negotiations. Theorin is emerging as one of the most clearheaded, outspoken, and moral voices at the international governmental level.

She continues:

"No one can maintain with any degree of credibility that these enormous investments in military power have made today's world a safer place to live in." The eight hundred billion world military expenditure figure "is more than the total income of the one and one-half billion people who are living in the poorest countries. If this rate continues, military expenditures will easily pass the thousand billion mark before the end of the 1980s. These figures are so huge that we cannot comprehend them unless we express them in terms of other uses.

For example, the cost of one single modern interceptor aircraft would be enough to vaccinate three million children against all the most common children's diseases.

The cost of one single nuclear-armed submarine would pay the annual wages of hundreds of thousands of personnel in social services for the elderly."

World military expenditures are dragging down the world and national economies. Jobs, social programs, and economic growth and development are competing for the same resources as arms. Arms are winning. Even now we are victimizing ourselves by this insane fixation on and addiction to military "solutions" to complex political, economic, and sometimes religious conflicts. The growing gulf between the world's poor and wealthy is one of the primary threats to peace and security. Theorin summarizes it well: "The world is faced with a choice. It can continue the arms race at an undiminished rate, or it can try to create a more stable and balanced international economic order and a political system that has a chance of being durable. The world cannot do both things at the same time. It has to choose one or the other. The arms race and underdevelopment are not two problems. They are one and the same problem. They must be solved together — otherwise they will never be solved."

Conventional weapons developments and battlefield nuclear weapons, must also become part of the agenda for disarmament advocates. The sophistication and lethal nature of so-called conventional arms must be addressed in the search for security.

Technological and political developments have brought us to the final abyss. But we can still jump out of the nuclear boiling pot. There is not much time. Leaders in Washington and in the Kremlin continue to build nuclear weapons, advisers paint 'scenarios' for their use — the weapons that can never be used. Each increment of the arms race has only accelerated the likelihood that at some time deterrence will fail, if not through the miscalculation of world leaders, then by technical malfunction or human error.

But what about the Russians? There is no evidence to suggest that the Soviet Union considers nuclear war survivable. The Soviets are having to come to terms with the realities of nuclear war just as our leaders are. They realize that to use nuclear weapons would lead to an all-out exchange. It would be suicide. Nonetheless, nuclear weapons play the same political and military role for the Soviets as they do for the United States. The threat of nuclear war is the context in which the Soviets carry out their foreign policy and exert their influence internationally.

The Soviets are not about to unilaterally disarm. While they have made several proposals, their behavior is the mirror image of their adversary's. Neither side is willing to take an independent step to break the deadlock and challenge the other. Neither side is willing to step back from its reliance on nuclear weapons for power in the world community. The Soviets see an "American threat." The Eastern Bloc countries are bolting from the tight grasp of the Soviet Union. China threatens them on one border, and economic and social problems at home challenge Soviet leaders, who are aware they were not chosen by their populations. "Solidarity" in Poland

and emerging independent peace movements in Hungary, Czechoslovakia, East Germany and the Soviet Union raise an unsettling voice against Soviet militarism.

Soviet insecurities make them all the more unpredictable and therefore dangerous to the security of the world. Any nation, including our own, that has enough nuclear weapons to blow the world up several times over has to be viewed as a threat. In fact, the Soviet Union has a vast military-industrial complex of its own, with its own peculiar features. There are hawkish, hardline voices within the Soviet Union competing for prominence and influence over Soviet foreign policy. These voices are reinforced by hawkish behavior and policies in the West. Soviet repression of their own people increases as pressures from without and hostilities with the West increase.

In too many ways the United States and the Soviet Union are mirror images of one another. The global role of the United States reveals a pattern of support for military dictatorships and repressive regimes that allows little room for criticizing the record of the Soviets. In our own country, the more we rail against the injustices in Soviet society, the more we seem to imitate and adopt its behavior. In recent years we have come very close to undermining our own democracy as we become more virulently opposed to the unacceptable in the Soviet Union.

Thomas Merton wrote in the early 1960s: "Far from producing the promised "nuclear stalemate" and the "balance of terror" on which we are trying to construct an improbable peace, these policies simply generate tension, confusion, suspicion, and paranoid hate. This is the climate most suited to the growth of totalitarianism. Indeed, the cold war itself promises by itself to erode the last vestiges of true democratic freedom and responsibility even in the countries that claim to be defending these values. Those who think that they can preserve their independence, their civic and religious rights, by the ultimate recourse to the H-bomb do not seem to realize that the mere shadow of the bomb may end by reducing their religious and democratic beliefs to the level of mere words without meaning, veiling a state of rigid and totalitarian belligerency that will tolerate no opposition."

But we must oppose the arms race. We must resist all temptation to be apologetic for our vision and peace advocacy in the face of smear campaigns and attacks on partiotism. It is because we cherish our heritage and have great expectations for our country that we dare to challenge the insanity of the arms race. To expect something is to hope. And hope is the theological and psychological necessity for stopping the arms race.

There is reason for hope. The confusion and passiveness of the public, combined with the moral paralysis of the decision makers, is a prescription for doomsday. In 1984, however, we are seeing massive numbers of people in the United States, Western Europe, the Pacific, and, increasingly, Easter Bloc Countries lose their fear, break out of their neutrality, and challenge the superpowers. Millions of this tiny planet's inhabitants are longing for government's leaders to "jump out of the nuclear boiling pot." There is a rising sense that something must be done. The fundamental moral and spiritual issues have spawned a religious peace movement. Doctors, scientists, civil rights leaders, social workers, and nurses, among others, have become engaged in the debate about the future of nuclear weapons.

People are no longer willing to accept the conventional wisdom that there are no alternative ways to defend the freedom and values we cherish. Nonviolent alternatives such as are proposed by Ron Sider and Richard Taylor in the last chapter are being discussed.

The old strategies for dealing with the arms race need to be cast aside. They have shown themselves to be impotent. The history of arms control efforts has merely managed the growth of the arms race. Each side agrees to a new ceiling for the other's arsenal and approves enhanced technologies. The growth of the arms race is managed by mutual consent, but the arms race escalates. Both the United States and the Soviets come to negotiations with new technologies as "bargaining chips." At the end of the negotiating process we get more chips and no bargains.

U.S. weapons are repeatedly proposed as necessary to "bring the Russians to the negotiating table." Build up in order to talk about building down, arming for arms control brings more weapons, not less. The following represent serious initiatives that could end the arms race and start the process for creating world security:

• An American-Soviet freeze on all production, testing, and deployment of new nuclear weapons and delivery systems. Such an immediate, bilateral, verifiable halt to the arms race is a precondition for negotiations between the superpowers leading to any real reductions of nuclear arms.

• Independent, reciprocal initiatives that would start a disarmament competition between the superpowers. These could include one side announcing unilaterally its plans to stop all warhead tests for six months, challenging the other to follow its example. If the other side did not reciprocate, testing could be resumed.

• The situation in Europe is extremely dangerous and volatile. Each side should announce steps to reduce the confrontation. The United States should withdraw any newly deployed cruise and Pershing II missiles and announce its intentions to forgo any new deployments. This nondeployment posture would continue as the Soviets began dismantling their SS-20s on an announced schedule of reductions. Either side could take the first step and challenge the other to reciprocal action.

• The trilateral treaty on a comprehensive ban on the testing of nuclear warheads should be signed by the United Kingdom, the Unites States, and the Soviet Union immediately. This treaty would inhibit the technological drive behind the arms race, begin a process of reordering the research priorities within the scientific community. (Now about thirty to fifty percent or more of all the trained scientists in American work directly or indirectly on weapons of mass destruction.) The comprehensive test ban would also be a powerful inhibitor to other nations now contemplating entering the nuclear club.

• Proposals for nuclear free zones such as those outlined by Swedish Prime Minister Olaf Palme and others should be implemented in parts of Europe, including the Nordic region, Central Europe (East and West), and the Balkans. A Mediterranean nuclear free zone would greatly reduce the dangers in the Middle East.

• Economic conversion planning for both academic, scientific laboratories and factory workers should take high priority within each country. A conversion plan combined with cuts in America's military research and development budgets would be not only wise economic planning, but a significant confidence-building measure for disarmament negotiations following a comprehensive freeze.

There are many other specific proposals that can be promoted. There is no lack of ideas. There is only the lack of political will by those in power. It is not up to the experts and politicians to end the arms race. World citizens must create a situation in which they can do nothing other than act decisively.

As Maj. Britt Theorin has said: "This is not an area reserved for the politicians and the experts. The work for peace is a call to everyone, and therefore I say to each of you: Dare to rely on your feelings and your common sense and react in the ways you know best. Use your imagination! Write simply, exactly as you think. Every single letter is of importance. Write to the newspapers — write poetry! Draw, dance, sing, embroider, arrange peace camps. Wear a campaign badge.

Make the opposition conspicuous. Write motions and statements. And above all, learn more. You can talk to the people you meet every day, with the people at work, those you meet in the shops. Become members of organizations—in the movements that suit you best. Discuss the questions you know something about, talk to the members of your club or association. But above all, rebel! Dare to make demands! Shoulder your responsibility for peace."

Beneath the hardware and the numbers there resides an attitude about war that is the central problem for people of conscience and faith. We cannot only blame the hardware for the deadly predicament the human family now faces. What gives our leaders license to threaten the annhilation of the human race? What could possibly justify this act?

In the final analysis we have to examine the selfish and self-centered nature of our fixation with "national security." We are justified in defending our values and beliefs. However, our national security obsession and the protection of our "vital interests" have too frequently come to mean the denial to others of freedom, self-determination, and cultural identity. "Vital interests" can too frequently be translated "oil" or other raw materials and resources.

The United States and the Soviet Union will soon have to learn that the world is one in which they must learn to live with others as partners with a common agenda: survival and world security.

Realism and pragmatism dictate this agenda as much as the moral imperatives. Restraint in the face of danger seems a mature response. As Thomas Merton says, "It would appear more realistic as well as more Christian and more human to strive to think of total peace rather than of partial war. Why can we not do this? If disarmament were taken seriously, instead of being used as a pawn in the game of power politics, we could arrive at a workable agreement . . . . The task of the Christian is to make the thought of peace once again seriously possible. A step toward this would be the rejection of nuclear deterrence as a basis for international policy. It is immoral, inhuman, and absurd. It can lead nowhere but to the suicide of nations and of cultures, indeed to the destruction of human society itself."

6

WHAT ABOUT THE THREAT TO FREEDOM?

Kenneth Brown

The train itself seemed to symbolize two sides of our Soviet experience. The sleeping cars from Helsinki were labelled "Tolstoi," but the color was drab army green.

Seemingly in the middle of nowhere, customs officials and soldiers swarmed under, on top of, and through the train. Two solemn soldiers patiently unscrewed the metal ventilation grate in the ceiling of our compartment and carefully inspected the small area under the roof of the car. No *National Reviews,* not even a *New Republic.* Oddly, new Levis, other clothes, and gifts seemed of little interest to them. My camera case, the usual focus of attention at the United States customs, was untouched. Magazines, printed or Xeroxed material, and books, however, were targeted for scrutiny. Authorities confiscated Xeroxed song sheets from a woman traveling with us, but she was allowed to keep her Russian Bible. I was permitted the songs but not my small Bible. A confiscation form appeared, which they required my wife to sign. The Bible was meant for no one in particular but, since relatively few are printed annually in the Soviet Union, we knew that worshipers in one of the churches we planned to attend would welcome it.

At the Polish border as we left the Soviet Union, customs officials again showed no interest in purchases but quickly confiscated my address book, professional cards of people I had met, and even tape recordings of a Baptist church service in which we had participated.

The official was brusk. "Are you a capitalist, Mr. Brown?" He probably directed the question to me because I was carrying the group finances.

"Not a very good one," my wife quickly replied.

"Can you take books by Lenin into the United States? You

know that Lenin was against capitalism."

Later, the same officer, inspecting the belongings of a woman from Delaware, uttered a single sentence: "I don't want my son to have to kill your son."

"I don't want my son to kill your son either," she replied.

Nothing more was exchanged. After the long process of lifting each car separately by hydraulic jacks and installing different guage wheels (Stalin deliberately kept the tracks from matching to slow invaders from the West), our address books were returned, and the train moved toward Warsaw.

In Moscow, we had met with faculty from the "Department of Atheism" at the University. Our own interpreter, a former student there, arranged the session. I asked the professors why a customs official would ever confiscate a Bible, and whether a religious text posed a threat to their society. They were apologetic and replied that the officer was mistaken in his duty. Every society, they added, has such uninformed officials. When we pressed further about the general restrictiveness of their government, they appealed to us to understand their history. We should realize how far they have come and how much they have achieved.

"Give us time to work out our problems," they said. At least twice we heard: "We are so defenseless." Soviet people and their leaders live in much fear. Often, their apprehensions seem groundless from our perspective; they seem, to use Sanford Gottlieb's phrase, like "an elephant afraid of mice."

The confiscated Bible was all too characteristic. Bookstores, even the largest ones, display few Western political or economic publications.

One evening in Moscow twelve of us took taxis to a nondescript housing development where we had arranged to meet with members of the "Group to Establish Trust Between the U.S.S.R. and the U.S.," an independent peace effort of a handful of professionals to focus on the dangers of the arms race. Eight people awaited us in a small flat. In our mutual opposition to nuclear weapons we felt the warmth and oneness that comes to kindred spirits. We exchanged small gifts, photos, and peace buttons. We gave them Jonathan Schell's *Fate of the Earth* and marigold seeds from the Fellowship of Reconciliation's "Seeds of Hope" campaign. They described their efforts for peace through art and photo exhibits, and petitions.

What deeply impressed me was the heavy price these peacemakers are paying for their witness. One by one, the group described for us the harrassment they had undergone: demotions on false charges, loss of jobs, surveillance, mail interruptions, and loss of phone service. Some are still in prison, endangered by health problems. These people, it should be noted, do not consider themselves dissidents or anti-Soviet. They do not disagree with official Soviet peace propaganda. They merely wish to work in their own way, independently, for mutual trust. There is little room for autonomy of conscience in the U.S.S.R. when that conscience seeks expression.

Our meeting was conspicuously open. We tried to emphasize its nonsubversive nature. The twenty of us in one small room talked and snacked until after midnight, joined hands in silent prayer and reflection, and sang "Shalom." It was difficult to say goodbye to them a few days later when they appeared on the platform at the train station to see us off.

Basic rights that we take for granted are prohibited in the Soviet Union. A Baptist woman was sentenced for distributing "pacifist" literature. A teen-ager was sentenced to two years imprisonment for raising an Estonian flag on their national holiday. A radio announcer in Moscow was subjected to mental tests and fired for referring to the Soviet army in Afghanistan as "invaders."

Religious activity is also strictly supervised. In addition to the sects, there are fifty million Russian Orthodox Christians, and two million Jews in the Soviet Union. Every fourth Soviet is Muslim. There is a sizable Buddhist population in areas bordering other Asian countries. Churches are packed because the government has severely limited the number of active or "working" churches. Despite the restrictions, their faith is genuine. They know that to follow Christ means downward social mobility. They have counted the cost.

Soviet law allows for freedom of religion, as reaffirmed in the Helsinki Agreement. But the government attempts to exercise control of religious activities. If they are to be legal, all groups must be registered. Their governing committees and use of buildings must be approved. Their collections and use of funds and even sermon contents are sometimes monitored. Evangelism or, for that matter, any outside activity of a religious, social, or charitable intent is prohibited. Christians imprisoned for various types of religious activity are tried for "parasitism," "hooliganism," slander of the state, or "anti-Soviet agitation and propaganda." The latter is punishable by three to ten years prison, plus two to five years exile. The Soviet constitution obigates citizens to do military service. There is no official recognition of conscientious objection, although evidence exists that unpublished regulations may permit noncombatant service within the military.

Amnesty International knows of 193 persons who have been forcibly confined in Soviet psychiatric hospitals over the past eight years for political reasons. The actual number is believed to be much higher. It has learned of more than four hundred people sentenced to imprisonment, internal exile, or other punishments from 1975 to 1979. It believes the real number of prisoners of conscience to be much greater. Amnesty International has not heard of a single case in which a Soviet court has acquitted anyone charged with political or religious offenses. The numbers reflect a Soviet ideology that rejects the idea of inalienable individual rights. Rights are invested primarily in the group, and all individual rights are derivative. The Soviet constitution guarantees freedom of speech, press, and assembly, but that guarantee is conditional on the "interests of the people and in order to strengthen and develop the socialist system" (Art. 50). Citizens cannot seek redress on the basis of constitutional rights because courts deal with specific law codes.

In contrast to the strong affirmation of individual rights found in the early writings of Karl Marx and in the European Marxist tradition, Russian history and geography have perpetuated the insecurity, secrecy, and repression of the Czars. It has been asserted that democracy as we know it has played no role in Russian history, and if it was suddenly granted to the Soviet people, they would not know what to do with it. Gottlieb has said, "There is little evidence that most Soviet people resent the one-party dictatorship under which they live. Most of the population is apolitical and tends to accept authoritarian rule." Our individual rights tradition simply is not part of the Russian tradition, either before or after the Revolution of 1917.

•

Socialist societies counter with a second set of human rights that they argue is even more basic than ours: the fundamental right of every individual to obtain the basic needs of food, clothing, shelter, health care, and education. These "social rights," they believe, are basic to human dignity and the fulfillment of any aspiration. Philosophers call them the "positive freedoms." They are the measure to which the Muscovite professors were referring when they said, "We have come so far."

By our standards the Soviet Union remains a poor country. Their agriculture, food storage, and transportation networks are inadequate. Their centralized, bureaucratic, low-incentive economy is inefficient. Nevertheless, there are no Salvation Army soup lines in their cities, no beggars, no evidence of malnutrition. Elderly people do not die from loss of gas or electrical services. The unemployed do not wander their streets seeking jobs, charity, crime, or all three. The poorest of their urban poor do not eat cat food and garbage. Welfare families need not survive at the end of the month on watered gravy while their political elites insist that cheats dominate the food lines.

Soviets consider employment the key to personal dignity, a fundamental human right. In contrast the systematic unemployment of minority youth in U.S. neighborhoods, half of whom are cut off from jobs, represents the inequality of wealth and opportunity in capitalism. The bottom fifth of households together receive only five percent of the income, while the richest fifth, a few neighborhoods away, receive forty percent. Soviets argue that great financial inequality results in great legal and political inequality. Jobless youth in America often end up in our prisons, "dissidents" who have lost this second set of human rights. Considering our wealth, the United States has a long road to travel in providing social rights. The other path to greater individualism and pluralism, which the Soviet Union must travel, is also distant.

Health care is another right in the second set of freedoms. It is estimated that the Soviet Union spends far less for it than the United States does, but regional and district hospitals are intended to guarantee medical service free of charge, and as locally as possible. Over five percent of all Soviet citizens are involved in health care. Innumerable complaints are aired in socialist societies about economic problems. But seldom does one hear serious objections to the health care systems.

As tourists in the U.S.S.R., we found dental services at nearly midnight. An American woman, sick from strange food and strenuous night travel, sat on a curb in Moscow, hysterical. She was immediately attended to by concerned pedestrians who called for professional medical assistance. When the American refused to enter an ambulance, they hailed a taxi. She spent the night in a hospital under the personal supervision of a medical doctor and was delivered to her hotel the following day, complete with prescriptions — all, of course, without charge. Medical care, though less technologically advanced than in the U.S., is readily available. Some area hospitals in the United States even refuse emergency care.

•

East and West reflect two quite different sets of freedoms. One set draws from the Enlightenment and is beautifully expressed in the U.S. Constitution and Bill of Rights. The second set draws from the social theory of the French collectivists and from Marxism. Roughly stated, one emphasizes individual liberty; the other, greater equality of opportunity and wealth (although equal distribution was not an emphasis of Marx himself). Each superpower emphasizes its own strength and the other's weakness. Each attempts to ignore its own weakness and the other's strength. The Soviet Union maintains that it imprisons no one for acts of political or religious conscience. It attempts to repress evidence of its repressiveness by silencing political and religious objection. U.S. leaders, on the other hand, deny significant social problems by perpetuating the myth of equal opportunity and appealing to the American dream of individual success. Failure is blamed on personal rather than societal inadequacy. Often we deny our social problems by overlooking them. Public officials in the South Bronx obtained several hundred thousand dollars for the purpose of placing plastic inserts in the windows of abandoned buildings. The façade was improved. Our social and economic failures are concealed from expressway travelers behind the facade.

The importance of both sets of freedom for human dignity makes any preferential debate futile. Whether individual freedom or social equity should come first is academic, given our different situations. Two radically different histories and two stages of history confront each other. Both East and West are sick in different ways. We have separate though interrelated illnesses, different symptoms, and we require different medications. Because the seemingly congenital weakness of one society is the congenital strength of the other, we have much to learn from each other. We must move beyond defending either the Gulag (a term Alexander Solzhenitsyn popularized. It refers to the prisons or work camps of the Soviet system) or the ghetto to attack both. We must seek societies that protect individual freedoms while providing essential needs. We must be vigilant against political repression in Poland or in Chile. We must struggle against budget cuts for UNESCO or press censorship as equally grave threats to human rights. The principle underlying all types of freedom is the resolve not to violate the person or, stated positively, the fullest realization of human potentiality. Although it is impossible for us fully to escape our own cultural preferences, we need to recognize both the U.S. and the U.S.S.R. as protectors and violators of individual rights, though in radically different ways. Any attempt to weigh or balance relative strengths, as with nuclear arsenals, is like comparing prunes and figs. Both East and West uphold freedoms; both societies threaten freedoms.

•

Strong psychological mechanisms of denial and projection are at work in East-West relationships. We enhance ourselves by projecting our weaknesses—that shadow side of every self and group—onto the other. This other becomes the "enemy," the focus of evil in the world, the cause of all our problems. It is the old scapegoat phenomenon, and it explains not only Hitler but much of the contorted history of this century. Hitler's rise to power was no aberration. Ernst Becker observes that Hitler understood that people want above everything else "heroic victory over evil." He gave Germany a self-image of a superrace and projected onto the Jews the weaknesses Germans could not face in themselves. Then he proceeded to offer "victory" over those weaknesses by exterminating the Jews.

We Americans projected our weaknesses onto the Nazis and, having defeated the Nazis, upon the Soviets. When our President accuses the Russians of being willing to lie, cheat, or do anything necessary to achieve their goal, he projects the shadow side of our own national behavior. Our hatred of each other is, in large part, hatred of our own failures.

When I talked with Soviet citizens, I was impressed by the mirror images of our two peoples. Both societies see the ghost of Hitler resurrected in the other. Both countries feel themselves threatened by a fascist power alien to their own nature. Soviets and Americans share an important aspiration: a longing for peace. They both view their own gigantic military systems as intended solely for defense. Neither group believes it would ever use its proliferation of ICBMs, and it will reply that those missiles will never be fired except in defense of its own country.

World War II seems to have taught East and West alike that negotiations and diplomacy are treacherous and conciliation futile. Both societies are convinced that there is but one approach to security: "peace through strength," understood almost exclusively as military power. The ghost of Hitler, in this respect, is everywhere. "Even if we lose, we shall win," said Goebbels, "for our ideals will have penetrated the hearts of our enemies." The ghost of Hitler lives on, determining our priorities, our policies, and, perhaps, our similar fate.

●

Are the Russians a threat to our freedoms? Certainly they are not about to win the hearts and minds of the American people. No segment of Western society, not even our disfranchised poor, seem attracted to the Soviet model. No viable political movement exists that would trade our Bill of Rights for a welfare society. Even democratic socialism has little following at the moment.

Internationally, the Soviet Union offers little real threat, despite the dire picture some people draw of red arrows slashing across the globe. The Soviets have significant influence in countries that encompass five to six percent of the world's population and gross product, almost identical to their influence in 1945 at the beginning of the Cold War era. The Soviet model is unsuited to Third and Fourth World countries. Its centralized, bureaucratic, managerial style is inapplicable for developing economies, including its own. Even countries that undergo socialist revolutions remain heavily dependent on the West for trade and technology unless, as with Vietnam and Cuba, the West itself isolates them.

The Soviet Union's real successes in ideological export have been in those areas where U.S. military force has been used to oppose Communism. As a superpower the U.S. and the U.S.S.R. alike have attempted to extend their influence through both violent and nonmilitary means. The results, in terms of human freedoms, have been mixed. The Soviet invasion and subjugation of Hungary in 1955 resulted in the subsequent liberalization of that regime. The Soviet subjugation of Czechoslovakia in 1968 did not. U.S. invasion of the Dominican Republic in 1965 produced a democratic government. All too numerous counter examples exist, whether in Guatemala or the Philippines, in which U.S. intervention has benefited not freedom or human rights but repression and impoverishment.

American citizens often envision the "Russian" threat to freedom in a fascinating scenario. The popular misconception finds Russian foot soldiers occupying Peoria, Illinois, confiscating all privately-owned guns, and imposing a dictatorship of terror. This scenario, grounded in a World War II context on another continent, is so absurd as to deserve more analysis. It confirms the psychological need for an enemy, however unbelievable. The Soviets are even less capable of invading the United States than we are of invading the Soviet Union.

In contrast to the "power projection" abilities of the U.S. armed forces, Soviet military power is basically defensive in design. The Soviets have few and small amphibious craft, insufficient troop carriers for air or sea, a few thousand marines. It appears they would have to invade the continental United States by crossing the Bering Straits into Alaska, an improbability that our own military leaders obviously do not take seriously. Our real fear is of Soviet power elsewhere, especially in Europe. But our best Sovietologists, including Goerge Kennan and Averell Harriman, believe that the Soviets have neither the ability nor the desire to in-

vade Western Europe. Yet pervasive fear of Russian Communism
continues, in part, because without it the U.S. would need to
substantially reorder its own politics and economics.

•

Is there then any real threat to our freedoms from the Union of
Soviet Socialist Republics? The answer is an emphathetic, resound-
ing "yes"! The threat grows hourly. The most basic of human rights
and the prerequisite for all others is the right to survival. None
other is more important, not because survival alone is sufficient but
because all other freedoms are dependent on life itself. Fifty thousand nuclear warheads, now numerous enough to blanket both
continents in holocaustal fire and radiation, are deployed and programmed for use. We measure our guaranteed future in spans of
less than thirty minutes, the maximum delivery time of destruction
from one ideology to another. Placement of intermediate-range
Pershing II missiles in Europe, and Soviet response with sea-
launched warheads off our coasts, shorten our assured survival
time to less than six or eight minutes. If by design or accident the
doomsday weapons are triggered, all human freedoms will perish,
capitalist and Communist together.

Consider that six to thirty minutes. Human rights, either individual or social, will be irrelevant. Technology will dominate.
There will be no time for parliamentary deliberation and open
debate in the great political tradition of the West. There will be no
decision by Congress or by the Supreme Soviet Council. The extent
of democracy or the sanctity of the voting process will be irrelevant
to the programmed responses of NORAD computers. The ex-
cellence of national health care systems or the vitality of First
Amendment rights will not matter. Nuclear weapons have
transformed the quest for security into potential suicide. They are
the ultimate threat to all human rights. Our fear of the Gulag and
the Soviet fear of the ghetto lead us into a madness where, if
anything at all survives, it will be the worst of possible worlds: a
Gulag ghetto, more terrifying even than a Stalinized South Bronx.

If by some miracle the present insanity does not repeat the consequences of past arms races, our fixation on security as military
might remains the greatest single threat to freedom. World expenditures of two-thirds of a trillion dollars annually for military
spending results in a neglect of the most simple human needs. We
speak glibly of protecting freedom at the expense of 1.3 million
dollars a minute for militarism while thirty children die each minute
for lack of food and simple vaccines, and eleven million babies die
each year before their first birthday. The Third World suffers

most, but even the superpowers, or rather their citizens, pay dearly for misconceived security. The U.S.S.R. spent approximately 1.3 trillion dollars between 1960 and 1981 on arms but ranked twenty-fifth in economic and social performance. The United States during that period spent half a trillion more, amounts that stagger the imagination and that could have solved the most pressing subsistence needs of the world's entire human population.

Our set of freedoms, individual liberties, are also endangered by the progressive militarization of our society. The hierarchical and bureaucratic nature of the military, the growth of centralized control, the need for secrecy in high techology weapons, and the general growth of state power combine to overwhelm the individual. The moral relativism implied in using whatever means necessary to achieve objectives results in the violation of human rights at home and abroad. The drive for military superiority has erased concern about repressive regimes. We ally ourselves with some of the most brutal, undemocratic governments in the world. Both superpowers make pacts with dictators for the cause of freedom. We embrace terrorism in the name of law and order. We promote war in the name of peace. The militarization of our society can make us the mirror image of the society we oppose.

The evils that we embrace out of fear of each other finally overshadow any evils in the enemy that we oppose. As Anthony Ugolnik says, "It is the intense hostility between our two countries and the hatred we so glibly fuel that embodies an evil greater than that contained in either one of us." We respond to the violence of the Gulag with threats of even greater violence, rather than with its opposite: a reinvigorated, thoroughly democratized society. Our anti-Communism throughout the world is represented in floating cities of weaponry, omnipresent bombs in the skies, and potential genocide entombed beneath the seas. The irony is that, as Hannah Arendt has written, the presence of violence indicates the absence of real power. The huge guns of the battleship "New Jersey" incite in many Americans pride and patriotism. They suggest to me lack of influence and loss of soul. Our militarism is contradictory to the values it intends to defend. And the atom gave our generation an absolute power that engenders absolute corruption.

•

Christians and Marxists share an aspiration that is basic to both sets of freedoms: a commitment to human dignity. The absence of either individual liberties or social rights endangers the dignity of the person. The tragedy of the cold war is that self-righteousness on both sides blinds us from mutual enrichment. We can and must learn from each other something of our own weaknesses, and of the other's strengths. Self-knowledge is much of what we fear. But self-knowledge is necessary to save us from self-destruction. The tragedy of the cold war is that it polarizes us into opposites and prevents the creative blending of the best of both societies. Czechoslovakia and Chile are sad examples. Czechoslovakia in 1968 was a socialist society moving toward democratic pluralism. Chile, on the other hand, was a democratic society that moved toward greater economic sharing. Neither of the superpowers would allow this creative synthesis, the very synthesis needed if the race is to survive and dignity is to be achieved.

Part III

CAN CHRISTIANS TRUST RUSSIANS?

There is no fear in love, but perfect love casts out fear (1 John 4:18).

But I say to you, love your enemies and pray for those who persecute you (Matthew 5:44).

All this is from God, who through Christ reconciled us to himself and gave us the ministry of reconciliation (2 Corinthians 5:18).

Can we trust the Russians? What about those Russians? From a Christian perspective these may be the wrong questions. Perhaps we should first ask, "How does God want us to respond to Communism?" "What does it mean to love our enemies?" "How do we exercise the gift of the ministry of reconciliation?"

As a boy I remember a mass evangelistic rally in our city auditorium. The speaker was E. Stanley Jones, saintly missionary to India and friend of Gandhi. He was dealing with the Christian response to the challenge of Communism. I remember only one answer. Since Communism breeds on poverty and injustice, Christians should be even more concerned about these cancers than the Communists. So basic, but so ignored by most governments and churches.

For a response to the Communist issue, we asked a young Mennonite who with his wife spent the last six years sharing the lives of Christians in Yugoslavia, a Marxist society. Drawing upon their personal experiences, Gerald Shenk deals with the varieties and nature of Communism, varying responses by Christians, guidelines and questions that should be considered in discerning a faithful response.

The promise of the book subtitle to delineate a Christian response or responses to U.S.-Soviet conflict may appear utopian. Dale Aukerman may be a good person to try to make one. His life pilgrimage has been one of relating his conservative biblical faith to service ministries, lifestyle considerations, and global issues. He has been aware that the way of the cross to which we have been called is regarded as naïvely impractical in our violent world. In the shadow of a possible nuclear holocaust, however, Aukerman's biblical exegesis suddenly has become most relevant. We must learn to love and live with the Russians or perish.

So many of our responses make us like what we claim we op-

pose in others. Our system supports totalitarian regimes and unjust structures because we say conditions would be worse under Communism. Where do we find in the Christian message that we need to wait until others become Christian before we can. We need examples of possible Christian initiatives.

The contributors to the last chapter of this book are well-known religious and national leaders who have thought carefully and prophetically about the basic questions of the anthology. They were asked to translate Christian answers into concrete actions and policies. In no way, however, were they requested to suppress their faith commitments and basic presuppositions. Their essays speak inclusively, overlapping with other essays. Yet each offers something unique.

Sister Jegen and Bishop Matthiesen speak out of their heritage of spirituality in calling us to pray for individual Russians with the confidence that it can make a difference. In spite of the claims that we have nothing against the Soviet people, but only against their government, it is the people who will perish if we launch our missiles. In a similar way Jim Wallis urges us to see our neighbor in the face of a Russian.

At a symposium on "What About the Russians?" Senator Mark Hatfield derived an important lesson from the situation before World War I. The arms race had gotten out-of-hand to the extent that the assassination of an Austrian Duke by Serbian nationalists precipitated an irrational drift into a terrible and senseless war. Senator Hatfield believes this may be the case today. An event or a series of events could ignite the unthinkable, a nuclear exchange. Instead of the frequent references to Chamberlain's compromising stance in responding to Hitler before World War II, Hatfield's example from World War I may be more relevant for us. It is in this context that he makes a passionate plea on behalf of disarmament.

Following Hatfield's political analysis, Ron Sider and Richard Taylor appeal to us to take seriously the possibility of nonviolent alternatives to the arms race. Adapting their article in The Christian Century *(July 6-13, 1983), they suggest practical strategies to bolster the sense of security as an alternnative to our present dependence on weapons of mass destruction.*

We also secured excerpts from the powerful preaching of William Sloane Coffin, Jr. There are few who speak more eloquently and practically to the basic questions that so many pose. Though the excerpts deal with different topics, his summary statements constitute a fitting conclusion to this anthology.

7

HOW SHOULD CHRISTIANS RESPOND TO COMMUNISM?

N. Gerald Shenk

Paul Tillich on Karl Marx: "His name has become so potent a political and semireligious symbol, divine or demonic, that whatever you say about him will be used against you by fanatics on both sides"(in *the Christian Century*, September 8, 1948).

"The contest has developed into a life-or-death struggle" (Kurt Hutten, *Iron Curtain Christians* [Minneapolis: Augsburg 1967; German original 1962]).

"In the West Marxism is the most potent alternative to the old way of life . . . . We need to know Marxism because it is the most vital doctrine of salvation in the secularized West, and we must be able to reply to it" Klaus Bockmuehl, *The Challenge of Marxism: a Christian Response* (Downers Grove: Inter-Varsity Christian Fellowship, 1980).

My first inkling that theology might make a difference in the real world came at a very early age. Until then, I would not have guessed that what happened inside our Mennonite churches in Pennsylvania mattered at all to anybody outside.

A well-known radio preacher had aroused his supporters to protest in the streets in front of the Lancaster meetinghouse where my family had come for worship that evening. I must have been old enough to read, because I knew the signs and slogans the protesters carried were much more hostile than their behavior.

Surging past the pickets, our people inside that simple building were preparing nothing more unusual than a welcome for church leaders from a far country. We heard testimonies, prayed together, and learned of the life of churches in different circumstances. Some of the visitors had Germanic names, which for that audience was additional proof of their authenticity.

But going to church that night in Lancaster was a subversive activity, because the visitors were church people from Russia. For the professional anti-Communist in the street outside, that simple fact dictated a noisy response. But for me and for the people with whom I would identify in maturity later on, that event of Christian fellowship across racial and political barriers was cause for celebration! An Anabaptist declaration on the state, on the enemy, and on the church was enacted that night in a way simple enough for even a child to grasp. Little did I know that years of my later life would be devoted to sharing the life of churches in a socialist society. The challenge of interpreting the reality of the church above national divisions made the air fairly crackle with tension that night long ago, and the intervening decades have not made the task much easier.

How should North American Christians respond to Communism? The conflict between East and West in our century has dramatically shaped our perspective on international affairs. We are all involved in the political and economic aspects of the struggle simply because we participate in this society. Our next-door neighbors may sense their stake in the contest between capitalism and Communism without any reference to religion. What makes our response to Communism a *Christian* response?

Many of the responses urged upon us come more from economic, political, and military interests than from the concerns of an authentic Christian faith. The Marxists have seen many so-called Christian responses to Communism. It is often easy for Marxists to portray those responses as an ideological veil, a cloak of religious language thrown over the class interests of the group that pays the fiddler to play that tune in its religious variations. And too often this interpretation is at least partially correct.

In order to be more Christian in the way we respond to Communism, we need to discipline ourselves to pay less attention to the clamoring, short-sighted self-interest urged upon us in North America. At the same time we must listen more carefully to those whose intimate acquaintance with Communism has qualified them to show from experience which responses more adequately demonstrate the truth of the gospel of Jesus Christ in that encounter. I refer, of course, to our brothers and sisters who live as Christians in socialist societies. But before we evaluate some of the responses urged upon us as Christians, we must take a brief look at Communism itself.

To What Must We Respond?

Communism today has taken many different forms. Its true character is a matter of raucous debate among its most devoted followers. No two Communist societies have identical social and political orders. Both domestic and foreign policies vary widely from Albania to Poland to Vietnam to Yugoslavia.

We do ourselves a disservice if we insist on finding a single Christian response to Communism, neglect those differences, and treat all forms of Communism as a monolith. Such a tactic would only reinforce the hand of hard-liners within the Communist world. It would also miss many creative possibilities by ignoring the many changes that keep occurring in Communist countries.

Like the elephant of the fable from India, Communism can be approached from many directions. Some would urge us to approach an understanding of Communism by reading its classic doctrines. "Free education for all children in public schools," and "Abolition of child factory labor," proposed the Communist Manifesto in 1848. Even if these proposals sound less than dangerous today, the Manifesto remains a model of the persuasive rhetoric that has awakened new fervor for justice in many societies around the world.

A second approach would be to treat Communism as an ideology. Marxism arose amidst a largely decadent Christendom in a Europe wracked by difficult adjustments at the outset of modern industrialization. In its passion for justice on behalf of the oppressed and sweeping sense of historical development, Marxism is, these observers argue, greatly indebted to the Judeo-Christian heritage.

Others claim it could not have come to power anywhere if it were not for the serious defects that had crept into the practice of that same Judeo-Christian heritage.

On either interpretation Marxism as a system of thought still shows traces of the intellectual and historic environs in which it was born.

Yet another approach sees Communism as a political system, a world empire acting as a bloc with aspirations for the spread of revolution. On this view, we must be in direct economic and political competition with that empire, since we live in a different one. And this may accurately describe the economic and political activity of most North American Christians. But we must not derive our faith from our economic and political activity! This would be much more Marxist than Christian.

What is more, neither side of the vast geopolitical clash of these two dangerous empires deserves the unqualified support of Christian theology. We have seen too much already of the notorious ability of preachers and professors on both sides to bless for hire. Some Christian leaders today have turned back from earlier uncritical support of governmental policies, recognizing just how large a threat to human survival is posed by this conflict of two bitterly opposed power blocs in the age of monstrous nuclear overkill.

A fourth approach would also see Communism as a political system, but in terms of it being the ruling party in societies where Christians live. Christians who choose this approach must accord Communism the minimal dignity of considering it a legitimate part of the international order. On this basis, then, we can tackle such broadly human concerns as the realization of human rights and the Helsinki Final Act. As part of this agenda, we ask about the rights of religious citizens and the role of the churches as part of their society. Christians have mounted numerous international campaigns on behalf of others in the body of Christ, demonstrating the interconnectedness and solidarity of this body across all barriers of nation, race, and system.

A fifth approach to Communism has been most instructive and provocative for Christians. This treats the encounter between Christianity and Communism as a meeting of two faiths. We must not, of course, insist that Marxists accept our designation of their ideology as a secular faith. But for our own clarity we may usefully compare the two as ways of organizing experience, as sources of meaning for life, and as motivation for commitment to a cause. We can't understand "the deep appeal of the Marxist system unless we consider its powerful effect upon emotions that are essentially religious," wrote S. H. Beer. Where does evil come from? How can suffering be redeemed? What sort of future is worth working for? When will the victims of history win freedom? Marxism has its own answers, answers formulated without needing to invoke supernatural powers, but answers nonetheless. This is the aspect of Marxism that most rigorously challenges us to *be Christian* in our response.

In 1951, in the turbulence of early stages in the encounter, an East German pastor wrote:

> A new (Communist) religion, claiming the total cosmos as well as the inmost conscience of men, is being proclaimed from the rooftops and in the smallest rooms. Yet the six years we have heard it have only been able to make us more sure of the truth of God and more sustained by it. "The spirit and the gifts are ours through him who with us sideth." It is our growing experience that God's Word is like a hammer that smashes the greatest rocks. Who can but rejoice to be there when it works? A pastor in the West must long to come over to us, much as in the old days a young knight often longed for the day of his testing! — Johannes Hamel, *A Christian in East Germany* (1960).

How Have Christians Responded?

Christians have been caught up in almost every conceivable response to Communism. To keep the whole picture in view, we should look at some of the most typical responses urged upon Christians as *Christian* responses to Communism. Some of the later paths were explored only after earlier ones had been tried. Most of them continue right into the present, somewhere in the many places around the world where Christianity and Communism are found together. Whenever appropriate, we shall first look at the responses at close range, then check for related patterns among Christians who can only relate at a distance to the encounter with Communism.

1. *Anathema and political repression.* Long before Communists were in a position to crack down on their political opponents, they were themselves relegated to the fringes of society, often outlawed and exiled, harassed without mercy. The international workers' movement was up against the forces of established Christendom. Some of the harsh critique of religion in Marxist ideology may be due to the repression the authorities in so-called "Christian" states meted out to its founders. Whoever hopes today for the toleration of religion in workers' states must not forget the treatment of Communists in earlier societies whose public order was officially Christian. Christians cannot rest easy with totalitarianism of any sort, but integrity in our criticism of it obliges us to include a measure of historical self-criticism, too.

2. *Response in kind.* When the Communist movement did eventually come to power during the chaos at the close of World War I, it was only in a backward society very much at the fringe of European reality. The significance of the event can be measured in the fact that fourteen nations, including Sweden, Great Britain, and the United States, were moved to send troops to intervene in the civil strife as the Soviet Union took shape. Invasions failed, foreign troops were expelled, and Communists consolidated their power throughout the whole territory.

In the decades that followed, the raw violence of militant atheism was unleashed against the churches of the land, more vicious in some times and places than others. But militant atheism has never been without a matching militant anti-Communism in the West, which draws extensive support from circles of people who consider themselves at the same time to be Christian.

3. *To Flee or Stay?* Too many people in our century have been forced to flee their homes, abandon belongings, and join the waves of refugees. Not all who fled Communist countries were Christian, and not all Christians fled. When Christians are among those who

choose to leave, it may be for a variety of reasons, including economic and political. But the West in receiving them almost always interprets their departure from Communist lands as a matter of freedom, especially religious freedom.

We can only speculate about the effects of turmoil, chaos, and war in the decisions these refugees had to make. It is not fair to second-guess their choices. But we are singularly ill-equipped to understand the choices of those other Christians who *stay on* in their homelands, even though they are ruled now by Communists. American Christians imagine that any believers who could would flee Communism at the drop of a hat.

4. *Selective opposition.* Christians who live in societies Marxists have organized have been obliged to order their relations with the wider society in any of several ways. The options are not very broad, but clear differences are in evidence. Whether in opposition, competition, "inner emigration," or critical cooperation and dialogue with their Communist society, the intensity of their encounter with Communism should have our respect. We have much to learn from their experiences.

Christians have been able to oppose certain features of Communist societies, even though this has sometimes been costly. They may resist state intervention in the organizational affairs of the churches, as do the much-publicized "Reform Baptists" of the Soviet Union. They may speak out against the military training of high-school youth, as do many churches in the German Democratic Republic. They may publish critical reviews of the movies shown in local theaters, as the Catholic press in Yugoslavia often does. Many Christians seek ways to register their objection to the atheist curriculum taught in the schools. Unwelcome as this criticism usually is, it almost of necessity is combined with tacit acceptance of the sociopolitical order. By approving the duties of loyal citizenship, church leaders make room for the worship activities of their congregations. With time and increasing confidence, this expands to theological training for church workers, youth activities, publication of Christian literature, and many of the features we expect to find in "normal" church life. Most of this activity is limited to the ritual functions of the church and does not spill over into public spheres. As such it is tolerated and even facilitated by Communist authorities in every society of Eastern Europe except Albania, subject to some limitations to ensure its isolation from anything political.

Outside the "Communist world," Christian opposition to Communism is also selective. The same rural communities provide

Marines for fighting Communist influence in scattered hot spots and wheat to feed Moscow. Some kinds of Communism are promoted as friendly to our national interests, while others are denounced as the source of all evil. Labor unions in Poland are brave, ours are scorned for being greedy; opposition to Communism here has strange contradictions.

Unaware of this selectivity in their opposition to Communism, most American Christians stereotypically project onto Christians who live in Communist countries a thorough, total opposition to everything Communist. We are tempted to suspect any who have not kept the faith and been jailed for defying the authorities. We have in this regard become the victims of our own favored fictions and clearly need to pay more attention to true accounts of the life of ordinary believers in Marxist societies.

5. *"Inner emigration."* This telling phrase from East Germany describes many Christians who have wearied of the confrontation with Communism. Unable to flee to the West, they have eventually come to the begrudging recognition that the power equation in their society is firmly fixed. Refusing the social responsibility of their own commitments and often not invited to contribute independently to formulation of public policies, they simply withdraw from the struggles of public life. Intellectuals and foreign Christians may be free to keep up the din of critical encounter with Marxism, but ordinary church members just burn out. Pastoral care in these conditions is a delicate task, struggling to keep the church from collapsing inward on itself in private devotion of no earthly good, as the Marxists have long accused it of being.

This "inner emigration" is strikingly paralleled in the West by the apathetic ignorance of international concerns that runs rampant in some branches of the churches. The real world of events matters little to this form of piety, for its faith has reduced such affairs to mere figures in its apocalyptic puzzles, signs of something else. Responsibility for the fate of the earth (and living neighbors in it) is shrugged onto more secular shoulders.

6. *Critical cooperation.* Some Christians who live in Communist societies are not opposed to socialism. Atheism as part of the narrowly defined Marxist materialist philosophy will keep them from being accepted into Communist Party membership, but they are not opposed to other parts of the program, especially its social and economic organization. If not against this much socialism, are they *for* it, then? They will want to distance themselves from the crude anti-Communism practiced by some other Christians. Must they then lose their Christian identity and be submerged completely in the program

of the Communist Party? Or can they support parts of that program as Christians but reserve for themselves the right not to support some other parts that conflict with their faith commitments?

East German Christians formulated the phrase, but it describes churches in many different socialist societies: not *against,* not *of,* but *in* socialism. If their government is working for justice and equity in social relations, Christians have their own reasons for cooperating. If atheistic instruction is built into the school curriculum, Christians will provide their own perspective through their own instruction at home or in the churches. They seek to express their loyalty as citizens while governed by their allegiance to Christ.

Most Western Christians, in contrast, are not very aware of their own ways of balancing loyalty and criticism of public policies as Christians. We have become too accustomed to a compartmentalization of life, keeping religious and public spheres quite separate. Our expression of social and political responsibility is then less guided by specifically Christian commitments, relying more on a vague ideology of the "American way of life." The recipes for mixing loyalty and criticism don't translate very well from one system to another. But if we cannot comprehend the difficulty of combining them in our own situation, we should not so boldly judge the decisions reached by our brothers and sisters in socialist situations. At best, we can learn from each other how to avoid uncritical, unreflective cooperation with political structures that cannot be Christian, whether East or West.

7. *Dialogue.* The most visible creative encounters between Christians and Marxists during the past two decades have been the frequent gatherings for careful joint reflection on the bonds and barriers between them. Dialogue between Christians and Marxists in Europe springs from the objective conditions of life, which have thrown them together but have not yet enabled them to come to terms with each other with much integrity. Mutual distrust and suspicion often break down in such close proximity. And yet a close encounter of that sort is risky business also. Instead of the stereotypes and slogans of the past (e.g., "religion is the opium of the people" and "atheism must be immoral"), dialogue partners examine honest differences. Understanding increases, but nobody can pretend to blend the positions into a gray mixture of both sides. Under the sharp questioning of the other side, participants are stimulated to redevelop and refine their own positions, only to submit them for further review.

Both theory and practice on each side provide grist for the mill of dialogue. Key topics help each side explore the limits and possibilities, the bonds and barriers in their experiences together. For example, alienation and sin are categories in which human evil is addressed. Its origin and persistence in human affairs are differently interpreted on each side, but its reality cannot be denied. For most Marxists, evil is a term for the alienation that has set people against each other and cut them off from the satisfaction of authentic, creative labor. It is the evil of a disturbance in socioeconomic relations, which should be relieved by a drastic rearrangement of those relations, especially by the curtailment of private property.

Most Christians find alienation to be more profoundly a matter of broken fellowship with our Creator, and also with the neighbors God has given us. We experience sin as separation from God's redeeming grace, and also as a breach in the social fabric of human life. Just as most Marxists need a more adequate concept of radical evil in human experience, most Christians would not have recognized the extent to which alienation has taken shape in the structures of human society if it were not for the Marxist analysis. Human responsibility in the face of evil, then, is a primary theme for the ongoing dialogue.

History, freedom, transcendence, ethics, hope, and the future are among the chief themes Paul Mojzes identifies as central to the future of the dialogue. Concern for the human being, the search for peace, and the meaning of work are also on the agenda, which does not arise from mere intellectual curiosity but in the practical fact that Christians and Marxists live together in so many societies around the globe.

How Christian Are These Responses?

I must emphasize once more that it is difficult to judge other Christians for their responses to Communism. But it is crucial that we sort carefully through the options already explored to find the ones that best express our own faith when challenged by an encounter with Communism. The following questions can help us evaluate our responses and pull together the elements of a more adequate and faithful approach than we could express without reflection.

1. *How close?* Some would be all too glad to relate to Communism without ever meeting Communists. But the long-distance encounter is ever fraught with suspicion, mistrust, and even terror. Christians charged with love for neighbor and enemy cannot rest content behind the barriers that keep authentic interaction from developing. The stereotypes and caricatures that each side inherits from its past serve only to hold the other at a distance and let us

nurse our prejudices and past wounds. Critical cooperation and dialogue best meet the test of proximity. Constructive competition in practical matters can also bring Marxists and Christians together. In many parts of the world those who are actively expressing their commitment to the poor, seeking justice for the oppressed, struggling for more basic fairness in international trade relations, and pouring energy into useful development programs include active Marxists and active Christians. Urgency in the efforts brings people together.

Because of geographical limitations most North American Christians cannot expect to have firsthand encounters with Communist societies, nor even with Christians who live in them. But we need to be careful about forming our picture of the life of believers "over there" on the basis of novels and the reports of émigrés alone. Imagine a foreigner who knows all about Chicago through movies about Al Capone, or of Hong Kong through Bruce Lee movies. Such is our limitation if we have only one source of information on which to draw.

2. *What kind of Christianity?* Each response to Communism presents a different picture of the Christianity invoked to support and explain that response. Those who respond to the worst features of Communism show the same sort of Christianity that sponsored the medieval Crusades. If "Reds kill Christians," some want Christians to do the same thing. Militant atheism is matched by militant theism. Both are godless and desperately at odds with the standards for the rule of God Jesus Christ outlined in simple clarity in his inaugural program (Matthew 5-7).

Other responses more clearly embody a Christianity no less courageous, no less willing to sacrifice for its cause, but free not to inflict death and suffering on others in pursuit of its goals. Where its cause is more broadly conceived than mere self-promotion, this Christianity can be as strong in its motivation for seeking justice for the oppressed as is Marxism.

The powerful church, accustomed to wealth and privilege, falls back on every possible unholy alliance in its anxiety over the threat from Communism. Preaching justice only for the age to come, it betrays its own hope in that age by its fearful struggle for organizational survival in this age.

The church that knows suffering, on the other hand, does not shrink from the victims of history; it has a natural constituency in every society. Relying on the power of the gospel, it knows that real change in this age is not alien to its goals. This church embodies the dangerous memory that kings and empires come and go and so do the churches that were married to those systems, but the rule of God among the downtrodden goes on forever.

3. *How clear are our goals?* Will Communists see in our response the power of our love, or our love of power? The stakes in the encounter are even higher when both sides are willing to express exactly how they feel about each other and how they expect to relate to each other. Christians can choose to demonstrate care for their neighbors, love for their enemy, and solidarity with the oppressed. Or they may struggle to save themselves at the expense of others and panic in an effort to preserve their privileges. Two different paths are before us at all times in the encounter with Communism. We cannot walk both of them at once.

One Christian may respond to Communism by affirming the goodness of God's creation, solidarity with all creatures, and the importance of honoring the sacred gift of life. Another response seems to place paramount importance on the security of some and the survival of our own group at the expense of everyone else. No Christian should care *less* for believers than for the rest of the world, but the church exists for others, especially for those who have never known the Good News of life in Jesus Christ. Even while we work for the salvation of all, we must also genuinely care for the welfare of all.

4. *How much moral integrity?* Our response to Communism must extend the scope of the moral activity possible in the encounter. We must clarify for ourselves and our neighbors the nature of the ethical choices confronting us. Some approaches communicate an integrity and authenticity that gains the respect of others. Dignity shared is dignity gained. Even some forms of opposition to Communism can be handled in respectful, open disagreement. But other ways of opposing Communism amount to a sellout of a Christian's moral heritage. The same distinction must be made among forms of cooperating with Communists. Each response we choose must be evaluated for its ethical impact on ourselves, on Communists we meet in the encounter, and also on the relation of local Christians to their Communist society when they are affected by our response.

Western Christians have often argued that because Communists are godless, we need not observe their rules and regulations. Since they oppose religion, we are allowed to break their laws. This may be the only way to provide Christians there with the amount of religious literature we want them to have, for example. If Christians there and Christians here agree, why shouldn't our abundance supply their need? The practice of smuggling begins with Bibles, but it can easily be stretched to include electronic equipment, foreign currency, and even automobiles and spare parts for Christian recipients. Many layers of secrecy surround such operations; very quickly the Christians on the receiving end lose their best hope of public witness in their society — the open, upright life of those who walk in the light. The accumulation of gadgets for ministry will be the envy of the neighborhood, but they can also become the target of customs investigations. The moral standing of these Christians in the community is then eroded and their witness stigmatized for generations as dependent on foreign subsidy.

But those who smuggle also point out a magic way of escape: emigration to the West. This may further weaken the staying power of the local churches.

On the other hand, excessively subservient compliance with governmental restrictions can also reduce the scope of responsible action for believers in Communist societies. The prophetic tradition of speaking truth to power is not very well developed in most of those societies and the church traditions there. When they visit, Christians from abroad sometimes have the freedom to witness boldly but respectfully to Marxist officials.

Consistency of moral behavior during times of social crisis can be a most persuasive witness in such encounters. Children from Marxist homes and former Marxists themselves in certain parts of the world today (e.g., Indonesia and Ethiopia) are turning to the Christian faith because they have seen its radical love persist when revolutionary rhetoric ran dry.

5. *Is the church international?* Both Communism and Christianity contain strong impulses to be international, to rise above the particular differences that separate peoples in the modern world. But the realities of Eastern Europe, it is widely agreed, have frustrated both Marxism and Christianity with the persistence and even strengthening of nationalism at the expense of the larger ideological communities.

For Christians, the basic criterion must continue to be, "In Christ there is no East or West." This takes precedence over any local considerations. Our response to Communism needs to bear witness to the truth of the church as a supranational reality, a new humanity transcending the present sociopolitical configurations. Failing in this, we would diminish the integrity of our witness to fit our narrower interests. The body of Christ is wracked anew in each generation as one part inflicts injury on another at the behest of caesars of every sort. We have forgotten how to be astounded that Christians are killing Christians in Ireland, in the Falkland Islands and in Central America.

Several months ago during a trip to the Soviet Union I heard a Baptist pastor from the United States reassure a Baptist youth choir in Kazakhstan that when he reported home to his own congregation about his visit to their city, his church members would not want to send a bomb over to destroy them. Perhaps the beginnings need to be just this simple. If we can be moved to spare the cities of our world for the sake of the righteous, the churches may yet make a vital contribution to the efforts for peace and reconciliation in the danger zones of our world. James Will in *Must Walls Divide?* pleads for redoubled Christian effort in the ecumenical task of healing the nations of Europe. If our vision of the church extends beyond national boundaries, we may hope to influence the behavior of nations along those boundaries. Local expressions of Christianity must all be disciplined to point to this larger reality, the unity of the church across human barriers. Communism is a challenge that puts this truth to a rigorous test in our century. Our response to Communism should be a testimony to the oneness of the body of Christ.

Is it surprising, then, to look back at that childhood experience in Pennsylvania that first showed me a church relating to this task, and to find implicit in that event each of the criteria raised in this chapter? On second thought, it is with delight that I bring an adult perspective to bear on the same agenda our church was addressing decades ago. Continuity of faithful responsibility is both a privilege and an obligation. The shape of faithful witness will be recognizable in every age, even though it undergoes a thousand new interpretations. The concern of the church for others will bring it into close contact with those who suffer, who are the victims of human history, and who ache for news that is good. If the churches are willing to be servants, they will not insist on dictating the terms of their societies' power arrangements. They will not be blinded with short-term self-interest but seek the welfare of others both now and for the future. The clarity of their goals and the integrity of their moral stand will be measured by their identification with the liberating work that God's Spirit is already unveiling in human history. They will not shrink in fear from cooperating with Communists in what is noble and humane in the possibilities of the present, nor will they hesitate to point to a better way in human relations than the reliance on force and coercion. But they will not fear to turn the light of critical social analysis on their own reality, either. Both the insights and the tools of the Marxist critique can serve as important corrections to the easy self-righteousness that tempts all religious people. The strongest responses to Communism that Christians have been making thus far, I believe, include critical cooperation and dialogue. But the urgency of our age makes this inadequate, as a recent experience indicates.

Conclusion: A New Realism

For the past six years my wife and I were privileged to share the life of Christians in Yugoslavia. What I learned there went well beyond my study program, crowding new issues onto my agenda. Where are the paths of Christian responsibility in a society whose welfare is directed by Marxists? Are the possibilities for the churches in the present significantly different from earlier stages in their encounter with socialism?

In one important respect the encounter between Christians and Communists there is very privileged: it is not encumbered with the baggage of the struggle between the empires of East and West. Yugoslavia does not belong to either of the power blocs. Thus the insanity of that conflict does not pump so much poison into the relation of church and society.

Other conflicts do concern Christians in Yugoslavia. The legacy of interethnic hostilities within Yugoslavia is just as defiant of simple solution as are the East-West tensions. At present the Protestant churches are best positioned to bridge the gaps among Yugoslavia's constituent peoples, for they constitute the only religious tradition that has reached beyond the confines of single ethnic groups. If the churches can model the reconciliation of the gospel across these divisions, their part in the pluralist society of modern Yugoslavia is assured. The Yugoslav experience is an encouraging case study in the potential for Christians and Marxists as they encounter each other in responsibility for a given social setting.

But we must return to the response of North American Christians to Communism. What are the realistic possibilities here? I have been astounded since our return to North America at the number of "Iron Curtain Christians" to be found here. By this I do not mean refugees, recent immigrants. I refer instead to those Christians who have fit their faith into the confines of our national mythology, boxed into the neat categories of the conflict between East and West. For them the forces of good are ranged against the "empire of evil" along the boundaries marked by the Curtain. The reduction of this struggle to religious terms is remarkable, but it does not make it Christian.

If the rhetoric of radio talk-shows is to be believed, popular religion in our society is doing much more to reinforce the walls between East and West than to reduce them. Sometimes it seems to contain a most damaging confession: our kind of faith could not survive in a socialist order. Persecution may be beneficial for the churches in the East, but we couldn't handle it. The ring of fear is in the background as the faithful are roused to renewed patriotic fervor.

Some of the fear is fully justified, even though it betrays true Christian hope. Popular religion that is content to take its direction from national priorities has good reason to fear Communism. If such faith is wed to the "American way of life," it can only tremble at the threat of revolution and disruption in the international trade patterns on which our lifestyle depends. The instant popularity of the war on Grenada was explained in part by the amount of American trade that flows through the region, making it an area vital to our interests, like the Mideast, the Indian Ocean, the Persian Gulf, canals, and seabeds.

A military chaplain offered consolation for Marines killed while battling island Communists in the Caribbean: they are now with God, he assured us, for they are "peacekeepers," and "peacekeepers shall be called the sons of God." Now that missiles have also been christened "peacekeepers," we can imagine some divine embarassment at all the paternity claims!

More soberly, the missiles point us toward the growing recognition that technological developments have overtaken us and finally outdated our narrow, partial concepts of security. The devastating scale of modern weaponry has suddenly made us one in a deadly and secular way, drawing East and West, North and South into a single destiny. History is set to render judgment on the crimes of nuclear preparation. We are all losing the arms race.

This is not the hour for handwringing, bemoaning the fate of the earth in advance. Nor can we indulge in idle speculation about how different the world would be if all Christians were Christian. It is still true that "if the Christian church in our generation could truly incarnate the Word of God and the gospel of Christ in its own fellowship and service, it would become the most powerful revolutionary force on our globe . . . . Marxism, which now challenges the church, would be mightily challenged by it."

But that was written twenty seven years ago! The world has changed much since 1957; by now we are almost beyond the challenges Marxism and Christianity can raise for each other. The urgency of our day is that both Marxism and Christianity are challenged to avoid the total destruction of the human race by the ripened fruits of the arms race.

On the day after a nuclear holocaust it will make absolutely no earthly difference whether Christians challenged Communism more effectively than Marxists challenged Christendom. More of the same old struggle is not the way out. We need a much tougher sense of reality than politicians and generals are offering if we are to see the things that make for peace (Luke 19).

New realism is demanded of us all, a realism that envisions a viable future for all. Present barriers can only show the limits of the order that is passing away, but we can use them as stepping stones to the age that must come. Christians and Marxists must meet at the ancient barricades if we are to see those barriers shrink under the pressure of the future. Paths must be made straight and relationships ordered according to a new reality. We must position ourselves to recycle the debris of the old as building blocks for the new order. The trash heaps of the old become the assembly points for the new.

We Christians have all the resources we need to take the first steps. The churches are invited to be revitalized by the tasks of making peace, forging the reconciliation that undergirds the only future worth having. Some are already experiencing this resurgent joy. For us the encounter with Communism is no longer a matter of reaction and defense. Communism has long been a challenge that tests our willingness to be *Christian* toward our enemies. Now we are challenged, together with Communists, in the test of our willingness to be *human* to all, to avert the extinction of the whole human race.

8

CAN WE LOVE THE ENEMY?

Dale Aukerman

In an Ohio church camp several years after World War II, a partly disabled German veteran told how a Russian peasant woman had saved his life. He was fleeing but had been so badly wounded that he could not go on. The woman took him—an enemy, a human being—into her hut, dressed his wounds, tore up her linen for bandages. After he had eaten and slept, he resumed his flight.

The German pastor, physician, and artist Kurt Reuber lost his life in Stalingrad. But in his last months he did a number of portrait sketches of Russians he had come to know. Those faces remain as moving expressions of a humanity shared amid the chaos and abysmal division of war.

Partly because of the ruthlessness of some Soviet actions and policies, partly because of decades of rigorously orchestrated propaganda, Western countries have a deep, prevailing fear of the Russians and, joined with that, immense animosity. The Russians on their side are increasingly gripped by fear of us, fear most of all that the United States will launch a nuclear first strike and destroy their country.

How, in a world that is careening toward nuclear war, can enough people see the human faces of those on the other side of the planet? In this dread time what can we learn from the biblical revelation about the Russians and ourselves?

One evening in the bitterly cold winter following the conquest of France—the winter of 1940-41—Magda Trocmé answered a knock at the presbytery door. Outside stood a frail woman with snow covering her meager clothes. She was visibly frightened. The marks of hunger were in her face and dark eyes. She said that she was a German Jew, fleeing from northern France, that she was in danger, and that she had heard that in the village of Le Chambon somebody could help her.

Magda Trocmé welcomed her in and fed her at the table near

the kitchen stove. As Philip Hallie tells in the book, *Lest Innocent Blood Be Shed,* that woman was the first of thousands of Jews who during those war years found their way to Le Chambon where Pastor André Trocmé and his wife Magda inspired and led the community-wide endeavor to hide them and help them across the nearby border into Switzerland.

To André Trocmé the Old Testament passages about "cities of refuge" (Numbers 35:9-34; Deuteronomy 4:41-43, 19:1-13; Joshua 20:1-9) provided a biblical background for these efforts:

> *You shall set apart three cities for you in the land which the Lord your God gives you to possess . . . . This is the provision for the manslayer, who by fleeing there may save his life. If anyone kills his neighbor unintentionally without having been at enmity with him in time past—as when a man goes into the forest with his neighbor to cut wood, and his hand swings the axe to cut down a tree, and the head slips from the handle and strikes his neighbor so that he dies—he may flee to one of these cities and save his life; lest the avenger of blood in hot anger pursue the manslayer and overtake him, because the way is long, and wound him mortally, though the man did not deserve to die, since he was not at enmity with his neighbor in time past . . . . You shall add three other cities to these three, lest innocent blood be shed in your land which the Lord your God gives you for an inheritance, and so the guilt of bloodshed be upon you.*
>
> (Deuteronomy 19:2, 4-6, 9-10)

Trocmé knew that people who did not deserve to die were being rounded up and taken off to be killed, and he had a clear obligation to go against the law and protect them. He and his coworkers took very seriously the biblical warning that if the innocent are slain in a city of refuge, the guilt of that bloodshed would be upon those who had failed to give them adequate protection.

Very few of us have ever answered that sort of knock. But far outside our doors are multitudes caught in a danger more awesome than the one that hung over the Jews in Nazi Europe. The little people of the Soviet Union and its allies may at any time be exterminated en masse by Western nuclear weapons. The converse is also the case: we in the West can at any time be obliterated by Soviet bombs. But we, like the villagers of Le Chambon, must do what we can to save the lives of persons about to be killed by the governments under which we live.

To be sure, one must face the issue of innocence and guilt.

Generally the millions of human beings sent to Auschwitz were not guilty of horrible crimes against humanity. Communists in their wielding of power have committed such crimes. Determined hostility toward them might then seem to be highly appropriate.

The texts about the Hebrew cities of refuge were concerned most of all with distinguishing between the innocent and the guilty. A person who had killed someone accidentally was to be given sanctuary and not handed over to be killed by an avenging relative of the slain person. But anyone found guilty of murder was to be handed over.

That differentiation received a strange reverse fulfillment in the trial of Jesus. The one who completely deserved protection from those intent on killing him was not given sanctuary. The Jerusalem oligarchy and the crowd handed over a completely innocent person to be crucified and rescued a murderer from the death penalty. Through that handing over, all the people involved incurred some degree of guilt for the shedding of innocent blood. And all human beings were implicated.

At the crucifixion of Jesus of Nazareth, the division between the innocent and the guilty fell in an extraordinary, new way. Only one was innocent. All others were guilty. "Cursed be every one who does not abide by all things written in the book of the law, and do them" (Deuteronomy 27:26 as quoted in Galatians 3:10). But that one took the guilt, bore the curse, died the death. It was, within the mystery of God's love, "life for life" (Deuteronomy 19:21).

A hymn addresses "you who for refuge to Jesus have fled," and that is an echo of Hebrews 6:18, "we who have fled for refuge." At the cross the guilty can become the innocent; God made Jesus "to be sin who knew no sin, so that in him we might become the righteousness of God" (2 Corinthians 5:21). This Jesus, who prayed, "Father, forgive them, for they know not what they do," this Jesus, risen from the dead, became the refuge, the sanctuary, the rescuer for any who came with whatever proportions of guilt and innocence to him. Those earlier cities of refuge have such fulfillment in him that none are to be handed over to human or divine vengeance.

If for ourselves we accept Jesus' taking our place and keeping the worst from coming upon us, we cannot—without flagrant incongruity—give others over to the threat or actuality of the worst on earth they might deserve. Those who have taken refuge in Jesus Christ become the new "city set on a hill" (Matthew 5:14). In the hearts of people of that city, refuge in Christ is given also to the leaders and masses in designated enemy countries; they are not handed over to be killed.

The Old Testament, in keeping with the avowed intent of the judicial system in any society, gives emphasis to the task of distinguishing between the guilty and the innocent. The latter are not to be condemned to death and killed. Only God can weigh the measure in which little people far removed from the levers of political power are guilty or innocent of dark deeds committed by their government and its agents.

Most Russians are even farther removed from those levers than are most Americans. Elections for them are still more weighted against decisive change in national leadership than are U.S. elections. It should be clear to us that in relation to the darker aspects of the Soviet system there is a rather wide segment of the Soviet population that is relatively innocent — and often more on the victim side. We should keep very much in mind that there are in the Soviet Union 50,000,000 professing Christians and 16,000,000 members of the Communist Party.

Correspondingly, an important element in the just war position has been the rejection of indiscriminate slaughter of civilians. But in the wars and cold wars of the twentieth century that distinction has become more and more illusory. It is profoundly contrary to the Old Testament concern for the relatively innocent and to the elementary wisdom of judicial codes around the world when nationalist passions and nuclear strategies consign entire populations to possible execution.

The grotesqueness of the current nuclear arrangements can be seen in relation to the people of Poland. There has been in the West broad sympathy for the Poles in their continuing resistance to Soviet-imposed repression. Yet in a Third World War it is probable that Western nuclear warheads would kill most, if not all, of the people of Poland (while Soviet bombs would be doing the same to the populations of Western Europe).

The Poles happen to live within the wrong military alliance. How preposterous it is when concern for them strengthens a reliance on weapons that can so easily annihilate them. The same considerations hold overall for the Czechs, the Hungarians, the Rumanians, the Bulgarians, the East Germans, and for wide ranges of the Soviet population, which is a patchwork of one hundred nationalities.

Beyond concern for the multitudes of relatively innocent Russians and Eastern Europeans, we can consider those who are more guilty and the way in which corporate guilt by complicity is shared by Russians generally. But then the mirror-image of all that is to be found on the American side. The great majority of both Russians and Americans give assent to a vast arsenal of nuclear weapons that at hair-trigger readiness could, even through some computer malfunction, bring death to hundreds of millions of people on the other side of the planet.

Even if we seek to resist the rush toward nuclear war, some portion of the darkness enfolding those arsenals is in each one of us. Dostoyevsky in *The Brothers Karamazov* observed, "In their hearts all men are murderers." It is possible that the nuclear arms race is a grotesque manifestation of Dostoyevsky's realism.

The New Testament moves beyond protection for the innocent to rescue for the guilty. The problem of evil is not centered in other persons, the other side, the enemy country. That problem for each person is centered in the person and in what is held to as "us." "Judge not, that you be not judged . . . . Why do you see the speck that is in your brother's eye, but do not notice the log that is in your own eye?" (Matthew 7:1, 3). "Therefore you have no excuse . . . whoever you are, when you judge another; for in passing judgment upon him you condemn yourself, because you, the judge, are doing the very same things . . . . 'None is righteous, no, not one'" (Romans 2:1; 3:10).

Sanctuary for the innocent is not enough. Each of us is in desperate need of sanctuary for the guilty. Because we have been given sanctuary in Jesus Christ, we are to give the Russians sanctuary in our hearts, minds, and actions. We do not leave them to their impending doom. We are ready to risk our lives in countering the terror that presses upon them. Beyond becoming a "nuclear free zone" with regard to what we look to for protection, we take up the task, by attitude and witness, of offering sanctuary, refuge, asylum to Russians. All their weapons cannot for much longer hold back that terror with its base among us from sweeping over them. They can have no effective civil defense. The most promising defense for them comes from communities of refuge here that disengage themselves from that base and extend love's domain.

Adolf Hitler described how his anti-Semitism developed as he walked the streets of Vienna: "Wherever I went, I began to see Jews, and the more I saw, the more sharply they became distinguished in my eyes from the rest of humanity." The most decisive element in his attitude was this setting of the Jews apart from the rest of humanity. Actually, all who were not Germans, Aryans, were seen as somewhat outside. But the Jews were focused upon as the epitome of those set off from humanity.

It is significant that for American English the most frequently used term parallel in form to *anti-Semitism* is *anti-Communism.* Anti-Semitism is directed mainly against people. Anti-Communism is usually thought of as ardent opposition to Communism as an ideology. But anti-Communism also is directed mainly against people. The ideology as such is hardly perceived as the threatening adversary, but rather the people who dynamically represent it. They come to be seen as apart from humanity.

In a society more and more overcome by hatred of the Soviets, what weight can we give to those Gospel passages that center in Jesus' command, "Love your enemies" (Matthew 5:38-48; Luke 6:27-36)? Jesus directed the imperative to "you that hear." The primary question is not what relevance this teaching has for U.S. foreign policy, but rather what directive it carries, if any, for American Christians in relation to the Russians.

It is commonly claimed that this teaching applies to personal enemies but can hardly be taken as applicable to national enemies. However, what Jesus gives as background for that command points in almost the opposite direction. He quotes Leviticus 19:18: "you shall love your neighbor as yourself," which is introduced there by the precepts: "You shall not hate your brother in your heart, but you shall reason with your neighbor, lest you bear sin against the sons of your own people." Neighbors were the fellow Israelites. There was to be no hatred toward or vengeance against persons within this ethnic and faith grouping. That formulation left the way open for the popular inference: one could rightly hate those outside this grouping or even outside one's own Jewish sect if it was seen as the only true Israel.

Some such division was implied in the question a lawyer put to Jesus with regard to the second great commandment: "And who is my neighbor?"(Luke 10:29). The rabbis had debated endlessly about who were to be excluded. In his reply Jesus struck down the popular demarcation between the in-group and those outside. For Jews of the time, Samaritans were the most hated and despised outside ethnic group.

Enmity between the two peoples had deepened over hundreds of years—intensified by incidents such as the destruction of the Samaritan temple on Mount Gerizim by a Jewish army in 128 B.C. and the desecration of the temple in Jerusalem by Samaritans who entered at night and scattered corpses. Jesus was a child when that defiling of the temple was perpetrated (about A.D. 6). For most Jews the deed must have come as infuriating confirmation of their darkest opinions about the Samaritans. One of the nastiest insults the Jerusalem adversaries of Jesus could direct at him was to call him a Samaritan (John 8:48).

In the command, "Love your enemies," the enemies Jesus reckons with are those who proceed as adversaries of the new people of God. They hate, curse, abuse the disciples of Jesus. The crucial division is not between the Jewish in-group and those outside but rather between those who have been drawn together around Jesus and those who see this new grouping as a threat and move against it. The division comes within the society.

But the hostile front moves only from the one side. Disciples are to face those adversaries with a love that takes shape in acts of good will, blessing as answer to cursing, and intercession for them. Love reaches out to overcome the division.

For Jesus the severest test of love comes when disciples are confronted by persecutors, not simply individuals who manifest a strong dislike for them, whatever may be the origins of that, but adversaries moving concertedly against them and the faith they seek to live. That is what enemies were for Jesus and for the early Christians. For followers of Jesus in many periods and places that is mainly what enemies have been.

American Christians generally do not, in a decisive way, have such enemies within the society. But the dominant fearful picture of who the Russians are and what they could do to us corresponds to the description Jesus gave of enemies. There is no Soviet persecution of Americans. But this possibility is seen as the great threat that military might must hold in check. What is feared is not so much a persecution of Christians but the prospect that the entire population would be dealt with in a fashion comparable to a terrible persecution of the church. The nuclear arsenal is seen as holding back the persecutors.

In the Stalinist decades there was widespread and violent Soviet persecution, and even wholesale slaughter, of Christians and other groups. Since then the modes of repression have become more restrained, and for most Christians and non-Christians in the Soviet Union life is more tolerable than most Americans suppose. But the critical issue is not how bright or dark a picture we have of Soviet society and Soviet intentions. There is much darkness in every society and government. Whatever degree of correlation there may be between American cold war images of Russians and who they are actually or potentially, to this degree Russians most of all are enemies Jesus tells us we must love. By and large we are not faced with nearby persecutors. If that command of Jesus in its central intent is to be seen as having any relevance for our present situation, then we are given the task of loving faraway persons who might incline toward doing terrible things to us.

Dietrich Bonhoeffer wrote: "And who needs our love more than those who are consumed with hatred and are utterly devoid of love? . . . As brother stands by brother in distress, binding up his wounds and soothing his pain, so let us show our love towards our enemy. There is no deeper distress to be found in the world, no pain more bitter than our enemy's." That applies when we look toward the darkness within the Soviet society—and within the United States.

The claim is sometimes made that one can go into battle loving the enemy soldiers or that there can be love for the Russians alongside a readiness to have and use nuclear weapons against them. However that may be in terms of mental acrobatics, Jesus was not talking merely about some emotional state of mind. He said, "But love your enemies, and do good" to them (Luke 6:35). That love is to be as forward and tangible in its expression as God's giving sun and rain to the unjust. *Agapé* is "a gracious, outgoing, active interest in the welfare of those persons who are precisely antagonistic." It is "being there for that other person before God." Such love cannot lay hold of rifle or hydrogen bomb.

Love of enemies is the opposite of our ordinary human response. But it is not some impossible ideal in an overwhelmingly lofty ethic. God loves that way and has loved us that way. We who live after the crucifixion of Jesus can contemplate a far greater wonder than the example Jesus pointed to: "While we were enemies we were reconciled to God by the death of his Son" (Romans 5:10). What should be overwhelming is not the ethic but God's love for us. And as we are drawn into marveling at that love and reciprocating it, naturally and without heroics our love will tag along with God's loving those who are most hardhearted and difficult.

The common translations of Matthew 5:48 with "perfect"—"You, therefore, must be perfect, as your heavenly Father is perfect"—are usually understood to express a call to be flawless, without error or sin. But behind the Greek word is the Hebrew *tamim* of Deuteronomy 18:13. God in loving is whole, undivided, all-embracing. As the New English Bible has it: "You must therefore be all goodness [toward enemies], just as your heavenly Father is all good." In the United States and around the world the chief and most decisive division that would delimit love is between our side and the enemy's side. But Christians, like God, are not to be divided and delimited.

Jesus does not ground his commands with regard to enemies in an expectation that they will be transformed into friends. In specific instances God may or may not succeed in bringing that about. For Jesus it is of prior and utterly crucial importance that disciples be transformed, that toward enemies they live the breakthrough of God's love into *their* lives. But this is so crucial partly because it can have a role in God's strategy toward those enemies — even as the obedience of Jesus, when his adversaries were closing in on him, was central for all God's purpose.

Jesus does call for a love toward enemies that is vibrant with expectancy. The unconverted love those who love them (Matthew 5:46-47). If persons they treat as enemies respond in love, this may possibly elicit love in return. But we can be filled much more deeply with a resilient hope for the enemy if we glimpse the wonder and dynamic of God's love reaching to the enemy and understand that God has overwhelmed even our rebellion. Only by grace are we enabled to love the unlovely as we realize that God loved us while we were yet sinners.

Western cold warriors, so many of them church people, tend to view the Russians as quite beyond hope. But this constitutes atheistic denial of God's living, loving sovereignty over the world. Love, also in looking toward the Russians, "hopes all things" (1 Corinthians 13:7). In the hilltop city there is abounding hope that enough light can shine forth to cause even Soviet Communists to "give glory to . . . [the] father who is in heaven" (Matthew 5:16). All this has decisive implications with regard to alternative approaches for relating to the Soviets. Confronted by the Russians and the call of Jesus, we can be sure that God in his purposes for them can better use our caring, prayers, and conciliatory initiatives than our animosity and hydrogen bombs.

How, concretely, are we to love Russians?
Discover them.

T. W. Manson commented about Jesus' reply to the lawyer in the story of the Good Samaritan: "Love does not begin by defining its objects: it discovers them. . . . The point of the parable is that if a man has love in his heart, it will tell him who the neighbor is; and this is the only possible answer to the lawyer's question."

It becomes increasingly clear that, without a turning back, the nations of the Western alliance will kill immense numbers of Russians. If we break with that momentum and stand against it, the Russians, of all faraway groups, become those we most need to see, reach out toward, and love. In this there are only two possible directions: We move toward annihilating the Russians, or we move toward caring about them.

George Kennan has delineated the alternatives in a different way:

> I would suggest that we try to repress what I fear is a peculiarly American tendency to what I would call the dehumanizing of any major national opponent: The tendency, that is, to form a species of devil-image of that opponent, to deprive him in our imaginations of all normal human attributes, and to see him as totally evil and devoted to nothing but our destruction.
>
> What I am saying applies, of course, first and foremost to the Soviet people. It is high time that we learned to see that people realistically, as the great body of normal human beings that they are—human beings like ourselves, struggling with their modest personal problems, with their individual triumphs and tragedies, trying to bring up children, to work out their loves and their aversions, to do the right thing where they can, and to search like ourselves for the meaning of life.

As Jesus went toward his death, he did not look only into the faces of friends and enemies who were within seeing distance. In his limited humanity he looked also toward all enemies and friends beyond that place and time. It is especially through him that today there can be the gift of vision that takes in the Russians.

Pray for the Russians.

Jim Wallis has pointed out: "Fervent prayer for our enemies is a great obstacle to war and the feelings that lead to it. Consider what might happen if the churches made prayer for our enemies a regular part of the eucharist. . . . If, every time we gathered for worship, we paused to remember and pray for the particular people our government has termed 'enemies'—how differently might we begin to regard our adversaries."

We could from time to time in worship make quite specific the most dangerous petition in the Lord's Prayer: "Deal with us in our wrongdoing as we deal with the Russians in their wrongdoing."

We can intercede for Christians over there, for Orthodox, Baptists, Catholics, Mennonites, Pentecostals, for underground fellowships, for Jews, for all harassed groups, for individual Russians we have met. Soviet leaders need our prayers as much as U.S. leaders do. We can strive to give over the deludedness of both sides into God's sovereign overruling.

Cry out for the Russians.

Bonhoeffer warned, "Only the person who cries out for the

Jews dare sing Gregorian chants." That crying out did not depend on knowing Jews personally or on having conclusive information about the concentration camps. It emerged individually and corporately from love's imaginative, empathetic vision of those multitudes under the shadow of death.

Christians in the struggle against the madness of nuclear weaponry must move beyond the natural and strategic focusing on what can improve the chances for *our* survival. Those trillions of dollars that are being offered up to the U.S. military go now most of all to develop a first-strike capability for starting and "winning" a nuclear war with the Soviets. Currently the incomprehensible threat to the future of humanity comes more from the United States than from the Soviet Union, not because the American leaders are more wicked, but because they hold with Promethean fascination a decided technological lead in nuclear delivery systems. But aside from the growing danger of an American first strike or a Soviet first strike out of fear that the United States is about to attack, that annihilation of hundreds of millions could be brought on by a computer malfunction, a miscalculation, a mental breakdown, or a terrorist act. We are to cry out for the Soviets and all East Europeans as we contemplate their extreme peril with and because of us. And we hope that more and more people over there will cry out for us and on our behalf resist the madness.

"Do good" to these "enemies": Work for the welfare and survival of the people of the Soviet Union.

Professing Christians have taken political power and proceeded by non-Christian norms with the general support of church people. In the nominally Christian West this pattern has undergirded the nuclear arms buildup. Without the prevailing assent of American churches, U.S. foreign policy and military posture could not have become what they are now. Were the churches to take a more prophetic posture, it could have and can have a significant impact.

The way of Jesus is that his people be salt and light and the new city (Matthew 5:13-14) in the midst of the largely unconverted world. If wider and wider circles within the churches in the United States and other Western countries disengage themselves from participation in the world arms race, stand against the nuclear delusion, look in loving concern toward the people of the Soviet Union, and call for peace and trade initiatives, such things that make for peace could be a weighty part of the political mix. What changes in national direction and international climate could come out of that only God in his sovereign mercy knows. We can live out the hope that the faithful witness of God's people may yet, under the Lord of history, be decisive for holding back the nuclear curse and bringing blessing to all nations.

9

WHAT CAN WE DO?

We Can Pray for Our Enemies

Sister Mary Evelyn Jegen, S.N.D.

To help us relate to the people of the Soviet Union, I want to suggest a simple exercise I discovered a few years ago. The idea came as a small group of us were praying together about the global issues of poverty and violence. In that prayer we experienced a call to a deeper commitment that was grounded in faith in Jesus.

From that prayer meeting I came away with the resolve to spend time each day in prayer with a picture of a starving child in front of me. At first I felt almost foolish, and sometimes restless. I resisted the temptation to grab for a book, even for the Bible, during that time, however. I spent it with God and that child. The exercise became painful and, finally, illuminating.

My suggestion for action to improve U.S.-Soviet relations is to find a picture of one or more persons from the Soviet Union. There are plently around in back issues of *National Geographic, Time, Newsweek,* or dozens of other magazines. I use a photograph of a five-year-old boy, Aloysha, and his three-year-old sister, Alexandra. They live in Moscow.

These two children now have a place in my heart, and I pray for them in a very explicit way. They are my brother and my sister. They are God's beloved children, as I know I am. He sent his own beloved Son into our world not only for me but also for Alexandra and Aloysha. Like me they have dreams and hopes, aches and pains, loves and fears, joys and sorrows.

They are our enemy. I don't let anyone tell me we have nothing against the Soviet people, but only against their government and against Communism. If we use our weapons, the government might fall, but Aloysha and Alexandra would burn and bleed and die. The truth is that if I do not resist the warmaking psychology fostered by so many in our country, I am in some way implicated in the state of enmity existing between the United States and the Soviet Union.

So I must resist. But I must do more. I must stir up my faith by looking daily into the eyes of this sister and brother. I am finding that I want to know more about them and their people — their way of life, their art, their literature.

I also want to express my love in practical ways. I want the Soviet people to have all they need, including international support for coping with the handicaps of their difficult geographical location.

I find myself praying also for the Soviet Premier and the American President in a new way. I pray that they will take time to look deeply into each other's eyes to discover the common fear of both peoples — and to take the risk of trust. I believe this can happen because I know the perfect love of God that casts out fear. I have learned it from my little brother and sister.

Are these glimmerings of a vision of active love foolish and impractical? Or are they part of a developing, new consciousness on which the security of our race will depend? There is no better place to test this question than in prayer.

"You must live your whole life according to the Christ you have received — Jesus the Lord; you must be rooted in him and built on him and held firm by the faith you have been taught, and full of thanksgiving" (Colossians 2:6-7, Jerusalem Bible).

We Can Change Perceptions of Each Other

The Most Rev. L. T. Matthiesen

We can change our perceptions of who the Russian people are and reach out to them in fellowship. These changes are imperative, not nearly so risky as our present passion for attempting to achieve peace through technological superiority. Antigun control enthusiasts remind us that not guns but human beings are the problem. Precisely. We human beings. We Americans (and the Soviets, too). More to the point: We Christians. We are the problem.

I think of Olga Korbut: Petite, impish, lovable. How we in the United States once loved her, admired her, applauded as she did her magic! We cheered and gave her flowers.

The memory of that nimble Soviet citizen has faded. The figure that skipped across our television screens is there no more, blacked out, blocked out, replaced by another image. The Olga

Korbuts have given way in our national consciousness to unsmiling Soviet negotiators, to graphs depicting Soviet superiority in conventional and nuclear weapons, to scenarios of Soviet tanks massed on European borders.

Has Olga changed? I think not. But our perception of her has changed. In composite, she is now untruthful, untrustworthy, unlovable. She is to be feared, hated, and destroyed.

What about the Russians? The question is rather, "What about us?" Have we not hardened our hearts? Is it not true that we have blinded ourselves, that we refuse to see Olga as she is in fact now — a human being, a sister, a wife, a mother?

The first imperative for us is to turn our hearts to flesh. We cannot selectively reject a portion of God's creation and call ourselves a religious people. If it is true to say that there is evil in the world — and it is — it is also true to say that it is everywhere. To declare that the focus of evil is in the Soviet Union is only partially true. We are in that focus, and to that extent we are citizens of the Soviet Union as well. The first imperative is to shun the sin of self-righteousness.

The greatest evil in the world is not atheistic Communism. The greatest evil is self-righteousness. Atheistic Communism delares that there is no God. Self-righteousness says that we do not need God.

The second imperative is like the first: Having been converted from our hardness of heart, we must reach out to the hearts of our brothers and sisters in Russia. No easy task, but possible nevertheless. Faith can move mountains. Faith can transcend barriers. Faith can break down the dividing walls of hostility.

It is, in fact, being done. Russian believers manifest their hunger for religious literature. The churches are alive in spite of some restrictions. Religion has only been scoffed at in the Soviet Union; it has not been eliminated.

The late Bishop Fulton J. Sheen used to say that one must reject Communism but love the Communists. Amen. Let us return to that attitude with renewed faith and hope.

We can reach out to our brothers and sisters in the Soviet Union in prayer, prayer that changes not God but us, Soviets and Americans alike.

We can reach out to our brothers and sisters in the Soviet Union in other ways, too, ways that are close to our hearts.

Who of us is not concerned about our health? And who would not be willing to take advantage of and share new discoveries, new surgical procedures, new treatments for cancer and other diseases?

An American doctor who saved the life of a Soviet child would do more for world peace than any terrorizing show of armed force could ever hope to accomplish. A Soviet surgeon restoring sight to a blind American would open our eyes to new possibilities of a lessening of conflict.

Who of us is not concerned about food, clothing, shelter, and transportation? Let us trade with the Soviet Union, do business with them, import and export, weave bonds of interdependence. The pipeline linking the Soviet and West Germany is more than a metal tube; it is a bringing together of people in a shared concern for energy, warmth, and light.

There is so much more that we can do: We can share technological development and engage in friendly athletic competition, cultural exchange, and mutual encouragement of the arts.

This presupposes communication and dialogue. Let us be ceaseless in our efforts to demand of the leaders of world governments that they extend to one another the hand of friendship, that they leave no opportunity for diplomatic encounter unexplored, that they abandon harsh rhetoric and reach out to one another.

The Olga Korbuts of the world deserve at least that much.

We Can Follow Jesus' Teachings

Jim Wallis

A group of Scandinavian women recently made a pilgrimage for peace by walking to Minsk in the Soviet Union. All along the way they talked to Soviet people who characteristically responded to their pleas for peace with words like these: "We want peace. But you know how the Americans are, we can't trust them. We can't let down our guard. If we showed weakness they would overwhelm us. The only thing Americans understand is power."

Another group of friends sat in at the Soviet embassy in New York as a witness for peace last summer. They were told the same thing: "We desire peace too, but the Americans are seeking military superiority over us. We have no choice but to continue to build up our military strength."

The words sound like a tape recording. Substitute "Russians" for "Americans," or vice versa, and you can hear it played over and over in every American and Soviet city.

Our respective national fears have become mirror projections of each other. Like most fears, some are real and some imagined. Both sides have behaved in ways that cause the other side to legitimately be afraid. Both sides have allowed their fears to escalate far out of proportion to reality. Both sides paint "worst-case scenarios" of the other and make the necessary preparations to meet them. Our fears have now made us comtemplate ultimate violence against each other, and unless dealt with, they will surely destroy us all.

While the arms race has many complicated political and economic causes, its root cause is fear. The bomb is the political result of fear, the logical, social extension of our personal anxiety.

Desiring to be saved from all the things that frighten us, we bow before our nation and its military might, which literally promises us salvation. We have allowed our faith and security in God to be overcome by fear, the greatest enemy of faith and its final contradiction.

But our Lord has some direct and simple words for us in this historical moment. Jesus said, "You have heard that it was said, 'You shall love your neighbor and hate your enemy.' But I say to you, Love your enemies and pray for those who persecute you" (Matthew 5:44).

For many the admonition to love our enemies is believable only as long as the enemies are general and unspecified. But when they are identified as Russians, Iranians, Cubans, or whomever the government names as our adversaries, the statement becomes outrageous. "Love your enemies" is admired as the word of the Lord until it is suggested that it means you can't simultaneously love your enemies and plot their annihilation.

"But what about the Russians?" continues to be the most commonly asked question when one begins to talk about the nuclear arms race. Even in the churches, the Soviet threat gets more attention than the words of Jesus. The question may indeed be the right one, but it is being asked in a tragically wrong way.

What about the Russians? What about the Russian people and their children? What would become of them in a nuclear war? They are among the hundred of millions of God's children whom we seem quite ready to destroy in the name of freedom, democracy, and national security.

The question we should be asking is, "What has become of us?" What does it say about a people when they are prepared to commit mass murder against "enemy populations," whatever the reason? For some things, there are no reasons good enough.

For thirty-eight years the Japanese have tried to get us to see their pained faces since the atomic bombings. But we have been afraid of what we might see: agony, shock, horror. To look is to have to face up to what we have done. To look is to see our future and our children's future written on their faces.

The devastation and horror we wreaked on Hiroshima and its sister city of Nagasaki are beyond imagination. The agony lives on in those who lost family members in the bombings, continue to lose them to cancer and radiation sickness, and discover the legacy of the bombings in generations of children who suffer genetic defects.

We have the capacity now to create 1,600,000 Hiroshimas, and every day we add three more bombs to our arsenal. We have come this far by not looking at the faces of the people of Hiroshima and by not looking at the faces of those we now call our enemies.

An Israeli soldier in Lebanon said of the people he was ordered to kill, "It's so hard when I'm up close. When I can see their faces, I can't bring myself to kill them. But when I'm farther away and am just shooting artillery shells, then I can do it."

A young American in a missile silo, one of many with his finger on the nuclear button, said, "I don't know if I could kill anyone up close. This way I never have to see who my missile hits."

Our missiles are aimed at the Soviet threat, the Russian system, godless Communism. It is certainly true that the Soviet system is cruelly oppressive. But missiles don't kill systems, they kill people—hundreds of millions of them. They will hit churches and kill millions of sisters and brothers who are one with us in the body of Christ.

It is a great historical irony that there were Catholics in the bombing crew that dropped the bomb on Nagasaki, the first and largest Catholic city in Japan. The ground zero target for the bomb was the Catholic cathedral. Among its victims were hundreds of worshipers and three orders of Catholic sisters.

The faces of Hiroshima and Nagasaki look at us quietly, patiently, earnestly, to show us the human face of nuclear war. They refuse to turn away from our eyes as we have turned away from theirs. They say, "See what you have done. See what is the fate of the earth unless you stop the mad race of nuclear weapons."

The words of Paul speak right to the heart of our problem: *But now in Christ Jesus you who once were far off have been brought near in the blood of Christ. For he is our peace, who has made us both one, and has broken down the dividing wall of hostility, by abolishing in his flesh the law of commandments and ordinances, that he might create in himself one new humanity in place of the two, so making peace, and might reconcile us to God in one body through the cross, thereby bringing the hostility to an end.*

(Ephesians 2:13-16)

At the time that these words were written, it was the Gentiles who were "far off." But today, when we think of who is farthest away from American Christians, we think of the Russians. They are the most feared, caricatured, unknown, inhuman to us. But the Russians have been brought near to us by the blood of Christ. The hostility God has put to death our government would stir up, and in so doing has directly set itself and our nation against the work of the cross of Jesus Christ.

The arms race will not end until we come to terms with the Russians. The nuclear freeze won't be enough; arms control won't be enough. Mutual fear and distrust will destroy us unless we overcome it.

Jesus never said that we would have no enemies nor that they would never be a threat. There is no lack of realism here. Jesus offers us a new way to deal with our enemies, a different way of responding that has the potential to break the endless cycle of retaliation that now threatens us all with ultimate violence.

In the past, Jesus' simple exhortation to love our enemies has been given a place of reverent respect and then summarily dismissed as politically irrelevant. Some theologians have called it "a necessary but irrelevant ideal." But the "realistic" approach has not worked so well. To continue to think that both real and imagined threats can be successfully countered with nuclear weapons is the height of unreality and naïveté. Nuclear weapons cannot defend us; they can only destroy us. In a time when all other solutions have brought the world to the brink of destruction, Jesus' plan for reconciliation may be our only viable option.

With the growing prospect of nuclear holocaust, Jesus' long-ignored teaching is revealed to be supremely relevant and vitally necessary. If we fail to see a neighbor in the face of our enemy, the consequences will be unthinkable. To ignore Jesus now, in the name of political realism, will allow our realism to destroy us.

Our perilous situation makes clear the mission of the church. We must step out, walk around diplomatic channels, ignore the obstacles, break the laws, and make friends of our enemies—American churches to Russian churches, American families to Russian families. We must build the bonds strong enough to defend both sides from nuclear weapons. And in so doing, we could make the words of Paul a prophecy for our future.

Honest Arms Control and Political Realism
Senator Mark Hatfield

Ten years after the atomic bomb had been dropped on Hiroshima, President Eisenhower expressed the frustration he felt over the momentum of the nuclear age. In a confidential letter to a friend he wrote:

> Today we are further separated from the end of World War II than the beginning of the twentieth century was separated from the beginning of the sixteenth century.

The nuclear phenomenon had compressed more than four hundred years into ten. This technological momentum adds immeasurably to the complexities that underlie the unremitting hostility between the superpowers.

Before we examine what motivates this antagonism, let us review the geopolitical landscape upon which both the U.S. and the Soviets now find themselves roaming partially blind. History can assist us in this review. For the geopolitical dynamic that proceeded World War I is a most appropriate parallel. The events leading to the outbreak of World War I tell us little about the consequences of a nuclear war, but they do shed an invaluable measure of light on the potential for its outbreak.

1. Austrian heir apparent Archduke Ferdinand was assassinated by Serbian nationalists.
2. Austria-Hungary used the occasion to renew its determination to absorb Serbia.
3. Russia was not about to accept another humiliation in the face of German threats to support Austria in this effort.
4. At the same time, "The savage cavalry charge of yelling Russian Cossacks became a fixture in European minds."
5. Armies converged on every frontier. No one was about to let his opponents get a headstart on the war.
6. The flow of world politics careened out of control and gave birth to decisions that ignored the ultimate consequences.

As those events unfolded, a young Winston Churchill was deciphering diplomatic cables and observed: "The terrible ifs accumulate." He could just as well have been reading today's newspaper. Israel is expected to continue to ask us for military hardware, including Pershing Missiles, to counter the new Soviet missiles. Every recent administration has refused to rule out the possibility of using nuclear weapons to protect "our oil" (I repeat, "our oil"). If nuclear weapons are used, there is every reason to believe that the strategic nuclear threshold will be crossed—in other words, all-out thermonuclear war.

In response to a massive Soviet nuclear build-up, we have employed Pershing II missiles in Europe capable of reaching Moscow in six minutes. The Soviet bureaucracy cannot possibly determine whether their computer screens are showing meteorites or missiles under that kind of time compression. The pressure for them to "launch on warning" will be immense. We are placing them in this situation even though faulty forty-cent computer chips have propelled us into false alerts many times. We are in effect sending a message to the Soviets that says, "We are so desperate to demonstrate our resolve to threaten you that we will entrust our very existence to your computers." Think about that irony.

I have outlined the risks of the present course so you can more effectively weigh the risks of an alternative course. For we are not posed with a choice between rational preparation and notions of pacifism. We are faced with a choice between the prospect of survival and certain destruction tomorrow, next month, or ten years from now.

We are told that it is useless to talk seriously with the Soviets about disarmament. We are told that, as a matter of doctrine, the Soviet leadership does not delineate between conventional and nuclear war and that it, in fact, pursues a policy aimed at winning a nuclear war. This is the excuse we use to justify the unprecedented surge in first-strike counterforce weapons such as the MX, the Trident II, the Midgetman, and the Pershing Missiles.

Are the Soviets more willing to risk conventional confrontation because they somehow do not see escalation beyond the nuclear threshold in the same apocalyptic light that we rational Americans do? I am convinced that the answer to this question provides vital insight into many of the other questions that surround Soviet intentions. We will not discover that they are angels. But we may discover that both superpowers are conducting a misguided search for excuses to rationalize their respective nuclear policies.

It is said that the Soviets rely heavily in their military doctrine on the dictum set forth by Karl von Clausiwitz, the nineteenth-century Russian warrior-philosopher. He said, "War is simply a continuation of politics by other means." The writings of Clausiwitz are then associated with the nuclear age by citing the opinions of more contemporary Soviet military strategists such as the late Marshal V. D. Sokolovsky, who asserted that "the essential nature of war as a continuation of politics *does not change with* changing technology and armament."

The implication, of course, is that the introduction of tens of thousands of nuclear weapons to the reality of warfare, with its promise of mutual suicide, does not change anything. Combine this with the Stalinist-Leninist imperative for world domination and the conclusion is derived that Russian Communism mandates a nuclear first strike.

This is the place where the nuclear gladiators, in my opinion, make their fatal error in logic. It is true that the Soviets give great weight to the teachings of Clausiwitz. But the apologists for U.S. nuclear superiority conveniently exclude a qualification set forth by Clausiwitz. He also maintained that war is not an act of blind passion. It is dominated by an objective. The worth of that objective must be weighed against the sacrifice employed to attain it.

In other words, if the Soviets desire to eliminate us through a surprise first strike, they would need to weigh their own total destruction against that goal. It is irrational, given current technology, to conclude that they would see that sacrifice in favorable proportion to the worth of their objective.

It might be well to examine Soviet ambitions as evidenced by some of their reprehensible behavior over the last two decades. If we honestly desire to understand the Soviets, we must delineate between Soviet adventurism and opportunism far from the homeland and Soviet actions closer to home, such as barbarism and oppression we have witnessed in Poland and Afghanistan. The former falls into the category of ideological struggle making life difficult for capitalism. The latter is motivated by inherited historic and nationalistic security concerns. The evidence strongly suggests that their nuclear policy lends itself to closer identification with Soviet border actions, that is, to deny access to a potential adversary, rather than as a desire to somehow conquer the capitalist world with a preemptive nuclear strike.

If we acknowledge the fears and the mindset that compel the Soviets to do whatever is necessary to maintain an impregnable buffer zone, their nuclear strategy should be seen in the following context. The better prepared one's armed forces are to fight and win a nuclear war, and the greater the success in implanting this fear in one's adversary, the greater the likelihood that the adversary will be deterred from striking first. Our thinking is much the same. As chairman of the Armed Services Committee, Senator John Tower has said, "I think we ought not to have a first-strike policy, but we ought to have a first-strike capability. And just as we do not judge Soviet intentions by their peace rhetoric, but on the basis of an assessment of their capabilities, so we cannot be surprised that the Soviets are quite justified in wondering just what we are up to."

The fact is that the United States has led the march in nuclear war-fighting technology. There are two principal components of a war-fighting strategy: multiple warheads and high accuracy. In 1970 we had an opportunity to ban multiple warhead missiles. As usual, we were short on foresight, even though we were far ahead in technology. We were not about to relinquish the advantage. The Soviets were interested because they were at a disadvantage. Now the Soviet accumulation of multiple warhead missiles haunts us and is cited as evidence of their desire to launch a first strike.

We have had numerous opportunities for a missile test ban that would prevent an increase in missile accuracy and dramatically reduce the confidence both sides need to contemplate a nuclear first strike. We have turned our backs on a comprehensive test-ban treaty that has essentially already been negotiated. The Soviets appear ready to sign. We are not.

It is amazing to learn of the type of arms control the moderates have demanded in return for their support of the MX missile. They have proposed a process known as "build-down" in which some number of old nuclear weapons (usually two) will be disposed of for each new one built. Supporters of the concept point out that, unlike the nuclear freeze, which would halt the testing, production, and deployment of any nuclear weapons on both sides, build-down would allow us to "modernize" (the new Orwellian term for escalate) our nuclear arsenal.

In other words, we will dispose of two old Volkswagens for each new Rolls Royce or Ferrari we build. Build-down is nothing new. Every so-called nuclear arms control agreement pursued by the U.S. and the Soviet Union has permitted both sides to build whatever new weapons systems they desire. This is but a new way to insure continuation of the old rules, namely, determine what you need (which is everything the weapons laboratories find promising on their drawing boards). Then a quantitative ceiling is attached to the agreement so you can call it arms control.

Having done this, the nuclear gladiators are free to ponder the next round in the arms race. Only the military in both nations benefits from this. In fact, build-down is a general's dream. It will permit every new first-strike system we ever planned while also allowing us to claim that the shelving of old weapons we had intended to dispose of anyway are gestures of peace. Under the terms of the build-down arrangement, the U.S. and the Soviet Union will be able to design nuclear war-fighting forces far more potent than what they possess today.

The term "freeze," on the other hand, accurately reflects the intent and substance of sincere proposals for arms reduction. The freeze implicitly treats technological strides in destructive capability as the preeminent danger of the arms race. The nuclear freeze rejects the worn-out Orwellian falsehoods that more weapons equal peace, that we need to "build-up" in order to "build-down," and that first-strike weapons are necessary for strategic stability.

Peacemakers can be instructed in seeing the parallels between the current political mind-set and the one that existed at the turn of the twentieth century. The peace movement grew strong during this period, just as it has today. The demand that governments make some serious effort to reduce armaments intensified. And just as with the build-down proposal of today, leaders of nations gave lip service to peace, while in truth they had no intention of themselves limiting the freedom to build all the arms they pleased.

As Pulitzer Prize winner Barbara Tuchman put it, "Political leaders told the public only what sounded virtuous and benign, while reserving the harsh realities for each other. Disarmament must be discussed, if only to prove to the public its impracticability and their own honest intentions." At the second international conference on arms limitation at The Hague in 1907, the leaders passed a resolution in twenty-five minutes calling for "further serious study" of disarmament.

They then settled down to serious work on the "laws and techniques of war" for six weeks. They agreed to meet again in eight years. Seven years later World War I had begun. Fortunately, they were not able to conclude the war in less than one hour as we are capable of doing today.

We can choose Armageddon, or we can choose the alternative: honest arms control and a political realism that holds no illusion about the dangers we face but places life itself above all other considerations. George Kennan has aptly said:

> For all their historical and ideological differences, these two peoples — the Russians and the Americans — complement each other. They need each other. They can enrich each other. Together, granted the requisite insight and restraint, they can do more than any other two powers to assure world peace. The rest of the world needs their forbearance with each other and their peaceful collaboration. They can have it if they want it. If only this could be recognized, we could . . . go forward to face the challenges that the true situation presents.

International Aggression and Nonmilitary Defense

Ronald J. Sider and Richard K. Taylor

The moral enormity of modern war is having an impact far beyond pacifist circles. Large number of Christians in the just war tradition believe the use of nuclear weapons would constitute murder. Many in that tradition have also concluded that even the possession of nuclear weapons is immoral and sinful. The World Council of Churches took this stance at its sixth Assembly in Vancouver in 1983. The vast majority of participants at the ecumenical conference on Life and Peace in Sweden (April 20-24, 1983) drew the same conclusion.

If the possession of nuclear weapons is immoral on the basis of the just war tradition, then just war Christians as well as pacifists are compelled today to seek nonviolent ways to defend democratic freedoms and national independence.

The extent of the "Soviet threat" can be debated, but it is incontestable that powerful nations regularly try to impose their will through military means. Biblically rooted Christians believe that "wars and rumors of wars" will persist and that "nation will rise up against nation" until Christ returns (Matt. 24:6-7). Political science joins this biblical view in a realistic analysis of the world's power struggles. History gives countless examples of one state's attempting to extend its influence by threatening another. Tyranny is far from dead. Some means of response has been and will be necessary for Christians to resist the spread of oppressive governments.

Few would argue that Christians should have stood by and done nothing while Hitler's Nazism was spreading. Few would dispute the fact that Communist leaders such as Stalin have exterminated millions. Realism suggests that immense threats to cherished values and institutions will continue to rise, whether in Soviet or some other guise.

The fact that American values and institutions are deeply flawed and that the U.S. sometimes acts oppressively in international affairs does not alter the fact that the current American system is preferable to any that an outside despot might try to enforce. "Government of the people, by the people, and for the people," though inadequately realized in the U.S., is preferable to government imposed by Soviet totalitarians.

Does this bring us back to "square one," the need to support military defense, even when "defense" with modern weapons involves us potentially in mass murder and the capacity to extinguish the human race? What if a means of defense could be found which does *not* rely upon military weapons, nuclear or conventional, and yet gives hope of protecting a nation's cherished liberties in the face of outside aggression? Such a means could serve as an alternative to military defense and war. Christians advocating defense of this kind would call not for disarmament but for *transarmament — transforming* the nation's defense system to one relying on nonmilitary means.

Even to pose the question sounds startling. A nonmilitary defense system sounds like a contradiction in terms.

But there are scholars, military experts, theologians, and peace advocates who believe nonmilitary defense to be a viable option. Its proponents include General André de Bollardière, one of France's most highly decorated generals, and Captain Sir Basil Liddell Hart, military editor of the *Encyclopaedia Britannica,* widely acknowledged as one of the foremost military writers of our time. Even the governments of several European countries (Sweden, Norway, Denmark, the Netherlands) have taken an interest in these ideas, studied them, and, in at least one case, run army exercises based on nonmilitary defense. Gene Sharp, an American proponent of such defense, has lectured at the U.S. Army War College. His writings on nonviolent response to aggression have received favorable reviews in several American military periodicals.

Proponents of nonmilitary defense point out that the current arms race is based on a "symmetric" strategy adopted by each of the superpowers. Each tries to match or surpass its opponent with weapons of the same kind — warhead against warhead, rocket against rocket, tank against tank. But successful resistance to outside tyranny has occasionally been mounted through an "asymmetric" strategy — pitting *non*military means against the opponent's military forces.

Such an asymmetric strategy was employed in Hungary's battle against Austrian rule in the mid-1800s. After crushing a Hungarian military uprising in 1849, Austria put Hungary under martial law, divided it into military districts, suppressed its parliament, and repealed its constitution. Militarily defeated, Hungary seemed to have no alternative but to submit to foreign rule.

Political and religious leaders, however, united in a strategy of absolute resistance without violence. They advised Hungarian citizens not to recognize Austrian rule and to treat Austrian officials as "illegal persons." Austrian decrees would not be obeyed. Hungarians would follow their own constitution and laws. Church services and government meetings would be held even when Austrian officials forbade them. Ferencz Deak, a Hungarian jurist and leader of the resistance, said, "We can hold our own against armed force. If suffering be necessary, suffer with dignity."

The variety of tactics used in the Hungarian resistance cannot be detailed here. Suffice it to say that Austria finally was forced to reopen the Hungarian parliament and restore the constitution. Hungary won complete internal independence. It resisted all Austria's attempts to destroy its churches' autonomy.

Advocates of nonmilitary defense are often asked if such tactics could succeed under a more brutal oppression. They reply by pointing to little-known instances of successful nonmilitary resistance to Hitler's demonic schemes. In Bulgaria, for instance, Bishop Kiril told authorities that if they attempted to deport Bulgarian Jews to concentration camps, he himself would lead a campaign of civil disobedience, lying down on the railroad tracks in front of the deportation trains. Thousands of Jews and non-Jews resisted all collaboration with Nazi decrees. They marched in mass street demonstrations and sent a flood of letters and telegrams to authorities protesting all anti-Jewish measures. Bulgarian clergy and laity hid Jews. Christian ministers accepted large numbers of Jewish "converts," making it clear that this was a trick to escape the Nazis and that they would not consider the "vows" binding. Because of these and other nonmilitary measures, all of Bulgaria's Jewish citizens were saved from the Nazi death camps.

Similar nonmilitary resistance in Norway prevented Vidkun Quisling, Hitler's representative, from imposing a fascist "corporative state" on the country. Finland saved all but four of its Jewish citizens from death camps through nonmilitary means. Denmark's asymmetrical resistance was so effective that Adolf Eichmann had to admit that "the action against the Jews of Denmark has been a failure."

The authors of a growing literature on nonmilitary resistance to tyranny are cataloguing and analyzing asymmetrical campaigns in many parts of the world and in various periods of history. These include the Indian independence movement led by Mohandas Gandhi, Germany's nonmilitary resistance to invasion by France and Belgium in 1923, successful Latin American campaigns to overthrow dictatorships by nonviolent means, and the recent Iranian revolution, in which massive street demonstrations overthrew the militarily powerful shah. A new organization, the Association for Transarmament Studies (3631 Lafayette Avenue, Omaha, Nebraska 68131), has been established to further these studies and to explore their relevance to the nonmilitary defense of the United States.

None of these historical examples, of course, proves that nonmilitary means can be substituted for military ones in the defense of a nation. But they do show that people have thwarted tyranny and defended their most precious values without violence or military weaponry. They point to a power to resist oppression that does not rely on the ability to kill and injure.

The success of nonmilitary movements cited is all the more remarkable when we consider their primitive and unrefined nature as compared with military defense. Most nonmilitary movements have not had the advantage of advance planning or preparation. A more carefully thought-out nonmilitary defense could perhaps produce even more powerful results, just as training and strategizing help the military to be more effective.

What do these historical examples say to us today, confronted as we are with the need to defend important values against totalitarianism and the moral and practical impossibility of defense with nuclear weapons? Perhaps they say we should be working not only for disarmament but also for transarmament. Perhaps we should be seeking a method of defending freedom and democracy that draws directly upon the nonviolence exemplified by Jesus.

How could transarmament come about? Public and congressional debate would first have to take place. Private and governmental agencies to carry out nonmilitary defense would have to be created, along with a plan for the economic readjustment that would come with conversion from military to nonmilitary defense. Military personnel and weapons industry workers would have to be retrained for civilian work. Large sectors of the U.S. population would need to be trained in the philosophy, strategy, and tactics of nonviolent resistance to aggression. Since American military weapons would no longer be available to protect vulnerable allies, they would need help in adopting their own nonmilitary defense systems.

How can those of us who reject a reliance on nuclear weapons for defense begin to work for an alternative defense system? First, we can educate ourselves about nonmilitary defense. (An excellent resource for study is the manual *U.S. Defense Policy: Mainstream Views and Nonviolent Alternatives.* Copies can be ordered from International Seminars on Training for Nonviolent Action, Box 515, Waltham, Massachusetts 02254.)

Then we can talk to people about nonviolent resistance as a moral means of national defense that has at least as much "practicality" as nuclear deterrence. We can persuade colleges and universities to do research on the topic. We can encourage public debate. We can urge nonmilitary defense upon political candidates and our representatives in Congress. We can form groups that use nonviolent means to attack existing social injustices. We can use nonviolent demonstrations to oppose specific nuclear programs while educating the public about an alternative means of defending precious values.

Would such an alternative defense system "work"? Can nonmilitary defense be justified on purely pragmatic grounds? Although it *has* worked in the past, there is certainly no guarantee that it will work in all circumstances. But then, the same can be said for military means of defense, which have their own mixed record of success and failure.

Would nonmilitary defense be risk-free? Certainly not. It would require a willingness to suffer and sacrifice. A population using it could well face imprisonment, torture, mass executions. But military defense also requires suffering and sacrifice, as the fifty million deaths of World War II so vividly illustrate. What if even five million people had been willing to die in a nonviolent struggle against Hitler?

Having nuclear weapons or not having them—both postures involve awesome risk. We face a chasm of uncertainty and risk never known before. For the Christian, obedient faith in Jesus Christ is the only bridge over the chasm. Does Jesus want us now to prepare ourselves massively to kill or massively to love our enemies?

On Trusting the Russians

William Sloane Coffin, Jr.

"What about those Russians? Can you trust the Russians?" It is well to remember that the same question is asked on the other side: "Can you trust those Americans?"

I suppose the first thing we ought to say, just to clear the air, is that we trust the Russians all the time on a whole variety of things. When the Russians want to buy eight million tons of grain, we trust them. We eagerly believe that is exactly what they want to do, and we trust that they will pay us as, indeed, they have paid us. If we know our history, we know that Churchill actually sent Stalin a congratulatory telegram thanking him for abiding by his word in not interfering in the revolution in Greece after World War II.

In other matters the Russians obviously have not been as trust-worthy. They did not observe the elections in Eastern Europe that they promised to observe. They have not encouraged self-determination in Hungary, Rumania, and other countries their troops occupied. The invasion of Afghanistan is certainly not a trustworthy act. And what they are doing in Poland is not par-ticularly trustworthy.

What we need to know is, can they be trusted when it comes to arms control treaties? The conclusion that is safe to reach, given our knowledge of human nature, is that all governments tend to keep treaties that are in their interest and to violate those that are not. The real question, then, is whether it is in the interest of Rus-sians and Americans to end the arms race. I do not expect govern-ments to be particularly moral, mine or the Soviet. I do hope they can be enlightened. So the all-important question is whether or not disarmament, properly supervised, is in everybody's self-interest?

On National Sovereignty

What has changed most fundamentally in the world is that the survival unit in our time is no longer a single nation or a single anything. The survival unit is the entire human race. The notion of absolute national sovereign power is as outdated as was the idea of states' rights when Calhoun proclaimed it and Jefferson Davis fought for it. That we do not see that simply shows how far behind the schedule we have slipped. This newfound oneness is the rediscovery of an ancient truth. From our perspective as Christians, we have always belonged one to another, everyone of us on this planet. This is the way God made us. Christ died to keep us that way.

On Dealing With Our Russian Enemies

The first thing we have to say as Americans, as Christians, about our enemies the Russians is that they are our brothers and sisters. It is not enough to say they breathe, they bleed, they have children for whom they have aspirations just as we have children for whom we have aspirations. No, we have to say they are our sisters and our brothers.

A second thing we can say is that while all of us are not guilty for this enmity, all of us are now responsible for doing something about it. We must deal with the all-pervasive enmity that is a part of the national psyche. How are we Christians going to love our Russian enemy brothers and sisters while at the same time we oppose their cruelty and injustice? This is not an easy task.

Here are a few suggestions when it comes to dealing with our Russian enemies. St. Augustine said, "Never fight evil as if it were something that arose totally outside yourself." This has great application in the public realm. Like the Russians, we Americans have intervened in the internal affairs of others — Iran, Guatemala, Dominican Republic, Cuba, Vietnam, and Chile, to name but a few. Generally we have intervened to make certain a country does not go Communist; the Soviets have intervened to make sure it stays Communist. Russian repression of civil liberties at home is dreadful, but surely no worse than the repression of these same civil literties that we aid and abet abroad. I am thinking of Latin America, the Philippines, South Korea, and Pakistan.

I picture a summit meeting coming off this way: The Soviet premier begins; "Mr. President, you have no idea of the terrible things we Russians have done." The president interrupts, "Please, Mr. Premier, you haven't a clue as to all of the horrible things I have done, not only abroad, but at home." In other words, confession is good in the national soul. If we are not one with the Russians in love, at least we are one with them in sin, which is no mean bond because it precludes the possibility of separation through judgment.

In international affairs, the importance of shame is crucial. If we Americans consider ourselves sinless and the Soviets the devil with whom you never strike a bargain, then we will never seriously negotiate. If we insist the only thing they understand is force, then we have to behave as if the only thing we understand is force. To quote Augustine: "Imagine the vanity of thinking that your enemy can do you more damage than your enmity."

On the Fruit of Fear and Enmity

All the poor and persecuted of the world, about whom we don't hear very much from our government these days, are victims of the worldwide greed for arms. We have to talk not only of the United States and the Soviet Union but of numerous Third World countries. The nations of the world spend $1.3 million dollars a minute on arms. We are talking about victims by denial. This is the fruit of our enmity, of our failure to think of the poor as our sisters and brothers.

On Love and Fear

The opposite of love is really not hatred but fear. "Perfect love casts out fear" (1 John 4:18). Fear is the real enemy that defeats us both as individuals and as a nation. The Indian author Tagore wrote: "The mind, seeking safety, rushes toward its death." Nothing scares me like scared people, unless it be a scared nation: a nation scared to death of Communism; scared to death even more perhaps of being soft on Communists. The following wise words were spoken by a British Foreign Minister shortly before World War I: "Fear begets suspicion and distress and evil imaginings of all sorts until each government feels that it would be criminal and a betrayal of its country not to take every precaution, while every government regards the precaution of every other government as evidence of hostile intent."

It is fear that continually enlarges the government's control over its population and that of its client states. It is fear that urges us to sacrifice freedom for security, to be more concerned with defense than with having things worth defending. So the first and the last enemy is always the enemy within. The last and first enemy is our own enmity, our hatred of others fueled by irrational fears.

On Peacemaking

We must negotiate an end to the arms race. Enough is enough. Arms control has always been arms control up; it has never been arms control down. When McNamara was secretary of defense, his concept was sufficiency. He did not care about parity, let alone superiority. Sufficiency was the all-important concept. Not anymore.

Proposals for a freeze recognize that the most lethal weapons are the new generation of weapons coming out with first-strike capability. I see nothing wrong with unilateral initiatives for bilateral disarmament. I feel the main problem is not our stated willingness to talk but our unproven willingness to disarm. The Soviets are on record time and again as saying they will sign a test-ban treaty tomorrow.

We need to engage in confidence-building measures, to exercise unilateral restraint instead of unilateral escalation. Hopefully we could get bilateral disarmament, then multilateral disarmament. When we establish a climate of acceptance sufficient to greatly reduce the nuclear threat, we could begin to reduce conventional weapons. The latter are only conventional in the sense that they are nonnuclear, not in the sense that they are nonlethal.

To reduce the risk of war with Russia, I think we should cease all kinds of warfare. I do not see any sense whatsoever, when you are dealing with the Soviet Union, to engage in any kind of warfare — economic warfare or psychological warfare. The idea that the Soviets are going to allow themselves to be defeated and are going to cry "Uncle Sam" seems incredibly naïve. Sensitive people on both sides are trying desperately to figure out what will happen next. If we are concerned for the dissidents, they will fare better when the atmosphere is not as charged. All dissidents, all homeless, all hungry will fair a lot better when the atmosphere is not charged with enmity.

On the Role of the Church

Religious institutions have important roles to play. It grieves me whenever I see churches retreating from the giant social issues of the day into the pygmy world of private piety. If Christ is God's love in person on earth, the churches ought to be God's love organized on earth. A deep desire for peace tempts some well-meaning people in the churches to be sentimental about Soviet policies and motives, while indignation at Soviet immorality tempts others to be reckless and militaristic. Both temptations should be resisted. Christians ought to remind Americans of the dangers of self-righteousness. They should remind Americans of our accountability to God and our responsibility before all human beings to continue life on this precious planet.

ENDNOTES

CHAPTER 1. WHAT ARE THE ROOTS OF TODAY'S RUSSIA?

1. I have borrowed this phrase from J. H. Billington, *The Icon and the Axe: An Interpretive History of Russian Culture* (London: Weidenfeld and Nicolson, 1966), p. 6.
2. See, for example, G. F. Kennan, *The Nuclear Delusion: Soviet-American Relations in the Atomic Age* (New York: Pantheon Books, 1982) and Richard Pipes, *Soviet Relations in the Era of Détente* (Boulder: Westview Press, 1981).
3. Daniel Bell, "Ten Theories in Search of Reality," *World Politics,* April 1958.
4. See X [G. F. Kennan], "Sources of Soviet Conduct," *Foreign Affairs,* July 1947.
5. F. Tiutchev, *Polnoe sobranie sochinenii* (St. Petersburg: Izd. T-va A. F. Marksa, 1913), p. 202.
6. G. F. Kennan, *Soviet-American Relations: The Decision to Intervene* (Princeton: Princeton University Press, 1958), pp. 13-14.
7. M. Gershenzon, ed., *Sochineniia i pis'ma P. Ia. Chaadaeva* (Moscow: Tovarishchestvo tipografii A. I. Mamontova, 1913), 1:74 ff.
8. Only portions of Western Russia (the principality of Novgorod and the part of Russia then controlled by Poland) escaped Mongol domination.
9. Richard Pipes, "Russia's Mission, America's Destiny," *Encounter,* October 1970, p. 3.
10. See Emanuel Sarkisyanz, *Russland und der Messianismus des Orients: Sendungsbewusstsein und politischer Messianismus des Ostens* (Tuebingen: J. C. B. Mohr, 1955), pp. 186 ff.
11. Billington, *The Icon and the Axe,* p. 78.
12. I. S. Turgenev, *Sochineniia* (Moscow-Leningrad: Izdatel'stvo Nauka, 1965), 9:167.
13. Cited from Hans Kohn, ed., *The Mind of Modern Russia: Historical and Political Thought of Russia's Great Age* (New York: Harper Torchbooks, 1955), pp. 46, 50, 57.
14. Hedrick Smith, *The Russians* (New York: Quadrangle Books, 1976), p. 467.
15. Nicolar Berdyaev, *The Origin of Russian Communism* (Ann Arbor: The University of Michigan Press), p. 7.
16. Ibid., p. 15.
17. W. S. Churchill, *The World Crisis 1918-1928: The Aftermath* (New York: Charles Scribner's Sons, 1929), p. 6.
18. *Izvestiia, March 30, 1934.*
19. V. O. Kliuchevskii, *Sochineniia (Moscow: Izdatel'stvo sotsial'noekonomicheskoi literatury, 1958), 3:12.*
20. Robert C. Tucker, "Swollen State, Spent Society: Stalin's Legacy to Brezhnev's Russia," *Foreign Affairs,* Winter 1981/82, pp. 414 ff.
21. Bertram D. Wolfe, *An Ideology in Power: Reflections on the Russian Revolution* (New York: Stein and Day, 1969), pp. 185-196.
22. Rolf Theen, "The Idea of the Revolutionary State: Tkachev, Trotsky and Lenin," *The Russian Review,* October 1972.
23. On persecution of the Russian Orthodox Church, see Gernot Seide, "Die Russisch-Orthodoxe Kirche in der Gegenwart: Rueckblick und Ausblick," *Osteurope,* November-December 1983, pp. 860-869.
24. Berdyaev, p. 15.
25. I. V. Stalin, *Sochineniia* (Moscow: Gosudarstvennoe izdatel'stvo politicheskoi literatury, 1949), 1:249.
26. Ibid., pp. 163, 164.

27. Ibid., p. 177.
28. V. I. Lenin, *Sochineniia* (Moscow: Partizdat TsK VKP(b), 1936), 27:417.
29. Ibid.

CHAPTER 2. ARE THEY ATHEISTS OR BELIEVERS?

1. Basile Kerblay, *Modern Soviet Society,* tr. Rupert Swyer (New York: Pantheon Books, 1983), pp. 248, 282. For extensive data on Soviet believers including more liberal estimates of their numbers see William C. Fletcher, *Soviet Believers: The Religious Sector of the Population* (Lawrence, Kansas: The Regents Press of Kansas, 1981).
2. Fyodor Abramov, *Dereviannye koni* [and other stories] (Leningrad: Lenizdat, 1979), pp. 39-40. The translation is mine.
3. Valentin Rasputin, *Farewell to Matyora,* tr. Antonina W. Bouis (New York: Macmillan Publishing Co., Inc.; London: Collier Macmillan Publishers, 1979), pp. 16-17.

CHAPTER 3. WHAT ARE THE PEOPLE REALLY LIKE?

"The Face of the Russian Church" was adapted in part from an article in *Sojourners,* November 1982, pp. 14-15.

CHAPTER 4. ARE THEY OUT TO BURY US?

"Two Views of the Soviet Problem" is an abridgment of an article in *The New Yorker,* November 2, 1981, pp. 54-62.

"The Myths of Soviet Intentions":
1. D. F. Fleming, "Can Pax Americana Succeed?" in *Struggle Against History: U.S. Foreign Policy in an Age of Revolution,* ed. Neal D. Houghton (New York: Washington Square Press, 1968), p. 273.
2. Ibid., pp. 275-6.
3. Fred Warner Neal, "The Cold War in Europe: 1945-1967," in *Struggle Against History,* p. 25.
4. Ibid., p. 25.
5. R. Joseph Monsen and Kenneth D. Walters, *Nationalized Companies: A Threat to American Business* (New York: McGraw-Hill, 1983), as quoted by John Kenneth Galbraith, "The Coming Invasion," *The New York Review,* December 8, 1983.
6. General Maxwell Taylor, *Washington Post,* June 30, 1981, quoted by *Washington Spectator,* September 15, 1981.
7. *The Defense Monitor,* Washington, D.C., 1982 (Vol. XI, Number 1), p. 9.
8. Ibid.
9. Anthony Lewis, "Reagan in Foreign Affairs," *New York Times,* July 17, 1980.
10. Fred Warner Neal, "The Cold War in Europe," in *Struggle Against History,* p. 37.
11. Ibid., December 20, 1983.

CHAPTER 6. WHAT ABOUT THE THREAT TO FREEDOM?

The author wants to thank George Lucas of the University of Santa Clara for making available excellent unpublished comparative articles on human rights in the United States and the Soviet Union. His article "The Inviolability Principle" appeared in *Encounter,* January 1984. An excellent edited series of articles is anticipated for *Soundings* during 1984.

CHAPTER 9. WHAT CAN WE DO?

"We Can Follow Jesus' Teachings" is reprinted from an editorial in *Sojourners,* November 1982, pp. 3-4, entitled, "What About the Russians?"

"Honest Arms Control and Political Realism" is taken from a speech Senator Hatfield gave at a symposium on Russia at Willamette University, October 27, 1983.

"International Aggression and Nonmilitary Defense" is adapted from an article in *The Christian Century,* July 6-13, 1983, pp. 643-7 and based on the authors' book *Nuclear Holocaust and Christian Hope* (Downers Grove: Inter Varsity Press, 1982), chs. 13-15.

Additional Readings and Resources

Aldridge, Robert C. The Counterforce Syndrome: Guide to U.S. Nuclear Weapons and Strategic Doctrine. Available from the Institute of Policy Studies, 1901 Q. St. NW, Washington, DC 20005.

Barnet, Richard J. The Giants: Russia and America. New York: Simon and Schuster, 1977.

Barnet, Richard J. and Crosby, N. Gordon. Moving Toward True Security. Pamphlet available from World Peacemakers, 2851 Ontario Road N.W., Washington, DC 20009.

Beeson, Trevor, Discretion and Valour: Religious Conditions in Russia and Eastern Europe. Philadelphia: Fortress, 1982.

Billington, J. H. The Icon and the Axe: An Interpretive History of Russian Culture. London: Wiedenfeld and Nicolson, 1966.

Cousins, Norman. "Of Russians and Americans" this and other articles are available from Promoting Enduring Peace, Inc., P.O. Box 5103, Woodmont, CT 06460.

Directory of Initiatives for U.S.-U.S.S.R. Reconciliation. U.S.-U.S.S.R. Reconciliation Program, Fellowship of Reconciliation, Box 271, Nyack, NY 10960.

Gottlieb, Sanford. What About the Russians? Published by Student/Teacher Organization to Prevent Nuclear War, Box 232, Northfield, MA 01360.

Holloway, David. War, Militarism and the Soviet State. Available from the Institute for World Order, 777 United National Plaza, New York, NY 10017.

Kaplan, Fred A. Dubious Specter: A Second Look at the Soviet Threat. Available from the Institute of Policy Studies.

Kennan, G. F. The Nuclear Delusion: Soviet-American Relations in the Atomic Age. New York: Pantheon Books, 1982.

Kerblay, Basile. Modern Soviet Society. New York: Pantheon Books, 1983.

Kistiakowsky, George B. The Arms Race: Is Paranoia Necessary for Security? Available from World Peacemakers.

Lossky Vladimir. The Mystical Theology of the Eastern Church. London: James Clarke & Co., 1957.

Occasional Papers on Religion in Eastern Europe, a publication of Christians Associated for Relationships with Eastern Europe (C.A.R.E.E.), an ecumenical association related to the National Council of Churches of Christ in the U.S.A.

Sawatsky, Walter. Soviet Evangelicals Since World War II. Scottsdale, PA: Herald, 1981.

Weingärtner, Erich, ed. Church Within Socialism. Rome: International Documentation and Communication Centre, 1976.

Wolfe, Alan. The Rise and Fall of the 'Soviet Threat.' Institute for Policy Studies, 1980.

Contributors

DALE AUKERMAN, scholar, graduate study in theology at the Universities of Chicago and Glasgow; author of articles in *Messenger* and *Sojourners* and author of the recent book *Darkening Valley: A Biblical Perspective on Nuclear War* (Seabury Press, 1980); peace minister in refugee camps, East-West contacts, International Friendship House (West Germany); itinerant peace evangelist and member of the staff of various peace movements (U.S.A.); member, Church of the Brethren.

KENNETH L. BROWN, professor of religion and philosophy and director of the Peace Studies Institute and Program of Conflict Resolution, Manchester College; frequent lecturer and author of articles on ethical and historical issues related to peace; Hiroshima Peace Walk and Atomic Bomb Conferences, Japan, 1977; director of "Journey of Reconciliation to the U.S.S.R., Poland, East Germany, and the Scandinavia," 1983.

WILLIAM SLOANE COFFIN, JR., chaplain of Yale University for eighteen years; presently senior minister of New York City's famed Riverside Church; influential religious leader and the prophet in the civil rights and peace movements; served in U.S. army as an infantry officer in Europe and a liaison officer with the French and Russian Armies in World War II; one of the initial advisors to the Peace Corps and first director of the Peace Corps Field Training Center in Puerto Rico; popular author and lecturer.

RICHARD DEATS, executive secretary of the Fellowship of Reconciliation; professor of social ethics at Union Theological Seminary in the Philippines, 1959-1972; ordained United Methodist minister; author of numerous articles and several books; leader of two peace journeys to the Soviet Union.

SENATOR MARK HATFIELD, United States senator from Oregon; former governor of Oregon; prophetic evangelical Christian; inspiring personal witness to applying faith to politics, in *Between a Rock and a Hard Place* (Word, 1976).

MARY EVELYN JEGEN, S.N.D., member of the religious congregation of the Sisters of Notre Dame; adjunct faculty member at Mundelein College and Creighton University; first executive director of Bread for the World Educational Fund; one of the founders of the U.S. branch of Pax Christi, the international Catholic peace movement; chair of the national council of American Fellowship of Reconciliation; popular writer and lecturer on spirituality and peace concerns.

GEORGE KENNAN, Institute for Advanced Study, Princeton; former U.S. ambassador to the Soviet Union and Yugoslavia; awarded Pulitzer and Bancroft Prizes for history; highly regarded author, lecturer, and authority on the Soviet Union.

THE MOST REVEREND L. T. MATHIESSEN, since 1980 bishop of Amarillo, Texas; former journalist and editor, Texas Panhandle edition of the *Register;* educator, rector of St. Lucian's Minor Seminary, 1962-1967; more recently peace bishop who has worked with his parishioners on the morality of working at the Pantex plant, at which the final triggers are placed on nuclear bombs.

CAROL PENDELL, second term president of the Women's International League for Peace and Freedom; leader of fourteen delegations to the Soviet Union; founder of U.S.A.-U.S.S.R. Citizen's Dialogue, Inc.; active in Methodist circles.

N. GERALD SHENK, doctoral student at Northwestern University and Garrett-Evangelical Theological Seminary with degrees from Eastern Mennonite College and Fuller Theological Seminary; recently completed a six-year assignment in study and service in Yugoslavia under the auspices of the Mennonite Church; member of Reba Place Fellowship, Evanston, Illinois.

RONALD J. SIDER, associate professor of theology, Eastern Baptist Theological Seminary; president, Evangelicals for Social Action; board member, Bread for the World; numerous articles and books, the latest with Richard K. Taylor, *Nuclear Holocaust and Christian Hope* (Inter-Varsity and Paulist, 1982); member of Brethren in Christ Church.

PAM SOLO, a sister of Loretto; on the staff of the American Friends Service Committee, 1973-1984; presently a consultant to their National Disarmament Program; one of founders of the Nuclear Freeze Campaign; travels extensively in Europe coordinating peace activity; academic degrees in theology and social sciences.

JOHN M. SWOMLEY, JR., professor of social ethics, Saint Paul School of Theology; former executive secretary of the Fellowship of Reconciliation; liaison in formulating nonviolent strategies with Martin Luther King in a civil rights campaign; member of the executive committee of the American Civil Liberties Union; president of the Methodist Peace Fellowship; author of many books and articles in social ethics, especially in the area of militarism and foreign policy.

RICHARD K. TAYLOR, self-employed author of numerous articles and books, the last being with Ronald J. Sider, *Nuclear Holocaust and Christian Hope* (Inter-Varsity and Paulist, 1982); served on the staffs of the Jubilee Fellowship Church, the Movement for a New Society, the American Friends Service Committee, and the Southern Christian Leadership Conference; cofounder of American Christians for the Abolition of Torture; Quaker-oriented activist who witnesses out of an evangelical faith.

ROLF THEEN, professor of political science, Purdue University, Lafayette, Indiana; scholar in Russian political thought and Soviet foreign policy; wrote the basic book on Lenin, *Lenin; Genesis and Development of a Revolutionary* (second ed.;

Princeton University Press, 1979); extensive travel and research in many countries including six trips to the Soviet Union; in 1967-1968, study for ten months at Moscow State University with research in archives in Moscow and Leningrad; on his last trip in 1981 he directed a two-week study tour of Soviet Union for twenty students; member, Church of the Brethren.

ANTHONY UGOLNIK, associate professor of English, Franklin and Marshall College; member, board of directors of the American Academy of Ecumenists; an American who has visited churches and traveled in the Soviet Union; published in religious journals and periodicals; places himself in the Russian tradition of lay theologians who approach religion from the affective dimension of literature.

PAUL VALLIÈRE, dean of University College and associate professor of religion, Butler University; formerly taught at Columbia University and served as chairman of the Humanities Program of Columbia College; expert in Russian mysticism and religion; periodic research in the Soviet Union, 1975-1977; recent book, *Holy War and Pentecostal Peace* (The Seabury Press, 1983).

JIM WALLIS, founder and pastor of Sojourners Community; evangelical activist in the forefront of movements for peace and justice; editor, *Sojourners* magazine; well-known speaker and social critic for church and academic audiences.

CLYDE WEAVER, director of marketing of The Brethren Press; twice religious publishers' representative to the Moscow International Book Fair; traveled extensively through the farmland of western Russia; presented over 160 slide programs as an expression of his interest in developing people-to-people contacts with the Soviet Union.

KATHERINE L. WEAVER, teacher for children with special educational needs; has taught sixteen years in the Illinois public schools; since she came out of a Midwest Anabaptist Mennonite tradition, her visit to Russia represented in large part a desire to search for her great-grandfather's ancestral home.